Apache Kafka
100 Interview Questions

X.Y. Wang

Contents

6 Guru 141

Chapter 1

Navigating the Kafka Landscape: An Introduction

In the intricate world of data systems, Apache Kafka has emerged as a pivotal player. Its prowess in handling real-time data streaming has made it an indispensable tool for businesses and developers alike. As the demand for real-time data processing grows, so does the need for professionals proficient in Kafka. This book is crafted for those eager to master this platform, offering a structured pathway through its complexities.

Welcome to your comprehensive guide on Apache Kafka interview questions and answers.

The essence of any interview is not just to test knowledge but to gauge problem-solving abilities, depth of understanding, and real-world applicability. Kafka, with its multifaceted architecture and vast capabilities, presents a range of topics that interviewers delve into. From basic concepts to intricate details, questions can span the breadth and depth of the platform.

This book is structured to mirror the journey of learning and mastering Kafka:

Foundational Concepts: We begin with the basics, ensuring a solid understanding of Kafka's core components and principles.

Intermediate Nuances: Building on the basics, we'll explore the more intricate aspects of Kafka, diving into its architecture, design decisions, and operational nuances.

Advanced Mechanisms: For those aiming for expert roles, we delve deep into Kafka's internal workings, touching upon its most complex mechanisms and features.

Mastering the Intricacies: The pinnacle of Kafka understanding. Here, we discuss the challenges faced in real-world scenarios, Kafka's integration with other systems, and the nuances of its design and operation at the highest level.

Each section is meticulously crafted, presenting questions that are frequently asked in interviews, followed by detailed answers. These aren't mere facts regurgitated but insights drawn from real-world applications, best practices, and the collective wisdom of the Kafka community.

Whether you're a budding enthusiast looking to start a career centered around Kafka, a seasoned professional aiming to switch roles, or an expert Kafka practitioner preparing for high-stakes interviews, this book is your companion. It's not just about preparing for interviews but about truly understanding Kafka, its place in the data ecosystem, and its real-world applications.

As you navigate through this book, treat each question as a learning opportunity, a chance to deepen your understanding, and a step closer to mastering Kafka.

Let's embark on this journey of exploration and learning. Welcome to the world of Apache Kafka interview preparation.

Chapter 2

Basic

2.1 What is Apache Kafka?

Apache Kafka is a distributed event streaming platform capable of handling trillions of events per day. Developed by LinkedIn and later contributed to Apache Software Foundation, it is designed to provide fast, reliable, and durable real-time data feeds.

At the core, Kafka is based on the principle of a "publish and subscribe" system for streams of records. It is similar to a message queue or enterprise messaging system. However, unlike traditional messaging systems, Kafka can retain and process streams of records in its platform – not just pass them from one end to another.

Kafka is run as a cluster on one or more servers that could span across multiple datacenters. The streams of records are categorized into what is known as "topics". Records sent to different topics are spread across Kafka clusters within a datacenter, with each record stored at a set of Kafka brokers (servers).

The key components of Apache Kafka include:

1. Kafka Producers: They publish records (push messages) to topics.

2. Kafka Consumers: They subscribe to topics and process the published records (pull and read messages).

3. Kafka Streams: Allows the building of applications and microservices that process the records.

4. Kafka Topics: A stream of records. Producers write data to topics from which consumers read.

5. Kafka Brokers: It is a 'server' in Kafka's distributed system.

A simple code example showing a Kafka producer and consumer in Java:

Producer:

```java
import org.apache.kafka.clients.producer.*;

public class Producer {
    public static void main(String[] args) {
        Properties props = new Properties();
        props.put("bootstrap.servers", "localhost:9092");
        props.put("key.serializer", "org.apache.kafka.common.serialization.
            StringSerializer");
        props.put("value.serializer", "org.apache.kafka.common.serialization.
            StringSerializer");

        Producer<String, String> producer = new KafkaProducer<>(props);
        producer.send(new ProducerRecord<String, String>("my-topic", "key", "
            value"));
        producer.close();
    }
}
```

Consumer:

```java
import org.apache.kafka.clients.consumer.*;

public class Consumer {
    public static void main(String[] args) {
        Properties props = new Properties();
        props.put("bootstrap.servers", "localhost:9092");
        props.put("group.id", "my-group");
        props.put("key.deserializer", "org.apache.kafka.common.serialization.
            StringDeserializer");
        props.put("value.deserializer", "org.apache.kafka.common.serialization.
            StringDeserializer");

        Consumer<String, String> consumer = new KafkaConsumer<>(props);
        consumer.subscribe(Arrays.asList("my-topic"));

        while (true) {
```

```
        ConsumerRecords<String, String> records = consumer.poll(1000);
        for (ConsumerRecord<String, String> record : records)
            System.out.printf("offset␣=␣%d,␣key␣=␣%s,␣value␣=␣%s%n", record.
                offset(), record.key(), record.value());
    }
  }
}
```

Apache Kafka is used in various use cases such as real-time streaming applications, data integration, real-time analytics, and mission-critical applications.

2.2   Who developed Kafka and why?

Apache Kafka was developed by engineers at LinkedIn in 2011. The team included Jay Kreps, Neha Narkhede, and Jun Rao. The primary motivation for Kafka was to solve the problems of real-time data ingestion and processing at scale which was a growing challenge at LinkedIn.

LinkedIn's infrastructure had to handle a huge influx of data from different sources (like clickstream events, application logs, system metrics, etc.). This data had to be made available to several applications in near-real-time for analytics, monitoring, and other uses. Existing solutions could not address these needs adequately. Traditional messaging systems struggled with throughput and durability. Log aggregation systems did not offer strong message delivery guarantees. Big data technologies like Hadoop were not ideal for real-time processing.

Kafka was designed to address these gaps. It combines the benefits of a messaging system with the storage characteristics of a distributed log system, and it's built for real-time streaming data. Kafka's unique design allows it to handle real-time data feeds with high throughput, low latency, fault-tolerance, and durability. These features make it an ideal choice for real-time analytics, monitoring, and event-driven applications.

Here are key aspects of Kafka's design:

1. Kafka serves as a buffer between data producers and data consumers, decoupling the data production rate from the consumption rate.

2. Kafka stores streams of records in a fault-tolerant, durable way.

3. Kafka allows consumers to read data in real-time or in a batched manner, treating real-time data as a continually updated batch.

4. Kafka ensures exactly-once processing semantics to guarantee that each record will be processed once and only once.

These attributes made Kafka a unique tool, capable of solving LinkedIn's critical data challenges. Soon after, Apache Kafka became an open-source project, and it is now used by thousands of companies worldwide for a diverse range of use cases.

2.3   What are the core components of Kafka?

Apache Kafka is a distributed streaming platform known for its durability, fault-tolerance, and low-latency capabilities. Here are the four core components in Kafka architecture:

1. **Producers**:

Producers are the entities that publish data to topics of their choice. They send records to Kafka brokers. Each record contains a key, a value, and a timestamp.

2. **Consumers**:

Consumer applications are the entities that read and process data from Kafka topics. Kafka keeps track of what has been read by storing the offset of messages. The consumers have the responsibility to commit the offsets. In case of Consumer failure, this offset is used to recover data.

3. **Topics**:

Topics are unique streams of records (aka messages). Each record within a topic is stored in a durable, fault-tolerant, and persistent manner. Kafka topics are multi-subscriber, meaning a topic can have zero, one or many consumers, each of which will receive all records written to the topic.

4. **Brokers**:

A Kafka cluster typically consists of multiple brokers to manage storage of records in topics for both publishing and consuming. Each broker can handle data for potentially thousands of partitions across multiple topics.

An example of a simple producer and consumer in Kafka is described below:

```
// Create a producer
KafkaProducer<String, String> producer = new KafkaProducer<>(props);
for(int i = 0; i < 100; i++)
    producer.send(new ProducerRecord<String, String>("my-topic", Integer.
        toString(i), Integer.toString(i)));

// Create a consumer
KafkaConsumer<String, String> consumer = new KafkaConsumer<>(props);
consumer.subscribe(Arrays.asList("foo", "bar"));
while (true) {
    ConsumerRecords<String, String> records = consumer.poll(Duration.ofMillis
        (100));
    for (ConsumerRecord<String, String> record : records)
        System.out.printf("offset_=_%d,_key_=_%s,_value_=_%s%n", record.offset
            (), record.key(), record.value());
}
```

In this sample code, we create a producer that sends data to the "my-topic" topic; then we create a consumer that subscribes to topics "foo" and "bar" and continuously listens and prints the data received from these topics.

Here is a diagram of Kafka's core components:

```
+---------+                    +--------+
|  Data   |                    | Kafka  |
| Sources | ---- Producers ---> | Broker | ---- Consumers ---> Sink apps
+---------+                    +--------+
            Publish records              Consume records
```

2.4   What is a Kafka topic?

In Apache Kafka, a Topic is a category or a feed name to which messages are stored and published. Essentially, it is a stream of records.

In Kafka, topics are always multi-subscriber; that means a Topic can have zero, one, or multiple consumers that subscribe to the data written to it.

Each topic in Kafka is characterized by the following properties:

1. **Name**: The name of topic which should be unique in a broker. It is used by producer for identifying the target of a message or data.

2. **Partition**: Kafka topics are divided into a number of partitions. Partitions allow you to parallelize topics by splitting the data in a particular topic across multiple brokers. Each message within a partition gets an incremental id, called the offset.

3. **Replication Factor**: Replication factor is the number of copies of a topic. Replicating topics ensures that data is not lost in case of a failure.

For example, a Kafka topic can be created using the command below:

```
kafka-topics.sh --create --bootstrap-server localhost:9092 --replication-
    factor 1 --partitions 1 --topic Sample_Topic
```

Here, 'Sample_Topic' is the name of the topic, 'replication-factor' is set as 1 (means one copy of data will be maintained), and 'partitions' is set as 1 (data is not partitioned).

Messages published to a topic are then distributed among the partitions of a topic. Each partition is an ordered, immutable sequence of records that is continually appended to a structured commit log. The records in the partitions are each assigned a sequential id number called the offset.

2.5   How does Kafka ensure fault-tolerance?

Apache Kafka primarily achieves fault tolerance through the replication of data. This means it duplicates the data to ensure that it is still available methodically in the advent of any failure.

More specifically, Kafka stores records in topics, and topics can be divided in multiple partitions, which can be spread over multiple servers (brokers) to balance load.

To make this fault-tolerant, we use the concept of Kafka Replication which means creating replicas for each partition. Record in topic will be replicated to 'n' number of Kafka brokers to ensure in case of broker failure it won't result in data loss.

Here is how Kafka Achieve it:

1. **Replication**: Each Kafka partition has one server acting as the "leader" and the remaining are "followers". The replication factor configuration determines the number of copies (including the leader) that are maintained. If a replication factor of 2 is configured, 1 additional copy (other than the leader) will be maintained by a follower.

2. **Leader for each partition**: A leader is a node responsible for all reads and writes for the given partition. Every partition has one server acting as a leader.

3. **ISRs**: Each partition has a list of servers that can be used to read and write data. This list of servers is called in-sync replicas (ISRs). For a follower to be in ISR, it should not lag behind the leader more than a defined number of messages/seconds.

4. **One Zookeeper quorum per Kafka cluster**: Zookeeper maintains the state of brokers, topics, and partitions. In case of broker failure, zookeeper notifies the failed events to the Kafka cluster, and the cluster re-elects the new leader.

Here's a brief illustration of fault-tolerance in Kafka:

Broker 1	Broker 2	Broker 3
Partition-1 (leader)	Partition-1 (replica)	Partition-1 (not replicated)
Partition-2 (replica)	Partition-2 (not replicated)	Partition-2 (leader)
Partition-3 (not replicated)	Partition-3 (leader)	Partition-3 (replica)

So, for instance, if Broker 2 fails, a new leader is automatically selected from the existing replicas in the ISR. The Kafka Producer and Consumer will not know anything about this change. Therefore, Kafka provides fault-tolerance if a broker or brokers have failed.

2.6   What is a partition in Kafka?

Apache Kafka organizes messages in different categories known as topics. Each topic is then split into a number of partitions. A partition is basically a fundamental unit of parallelism in Kafka and is an ordered and immutable sequence of records that is continually appended to - a structured commit log.

Let's understand partitions with the help of an analogy. Think of a Kafka topic as a book, and the partitions as the chapters of the book. The book is broken down into chapters to make reading, accessing, and managing the content of the book easier.

Each Kafka message within a partition is assigned and identified by its unique offset. A consumer can process data from a topic at its own pace and this is managed by simply note down the offset number. In simple terms, it marks an entry after reading the data by keeping track of the current position.

When Kafka writes data to a topic, it spreads the data across all partitions. The process by which Kafka allocates records to partitions is straightforward — it uses round-robin, going from partition 0 to N (where N is the number of partitions for the topic), and then back to 0.

Here is a simple diagram explaining how a topic is divided into partitions, and how each partition has different offsets.

Topic		
Partition 0	Partition 1	Partition 2
offset: 0	offset: 0	offset: 0
offset: 1	offset: 1	offset: 1
offset: 2	offset: 2	offset: 2
...	...	...
offset: N	offset: N	offset: N

One important thing to note is that communication between the producer and the consumer within a partition is strictly ordered. If you need to maintain the order of messages, a single partition can ensure this. However, using multiple partitions will only ensure the order of messages within each individual partition.

2.7   What is a Kafka producer?

A Kafka producer is a client or an application that produces Kafka messages and sends them to one or more Kafka topics. The producer is responsible for choosing which record to assign to which partition within the topic. This could be done in a round-robin approach, or a semantic partition function can be used.

Producers send records (key-value pairs) to a Kafka topic for processing. Each record consists of a key, a value, and a timestamp.

Here is a simple example of a Kafka producer written in Java:

```
import org.apache.kafka.clients.producer.*;

public class SimpleProducer {
    public static void main(String[] args) throws Exception{
        // Check arguments length value
```

```
if(args.length == 0){
  System.out.println("Enter⎵topic⎵name");
  return;
}

// Assign topicName to string variable
String topicName = args[0].toString();

// Create instance for properties to access producer configs
Properties props = new Properties();

// Assign localhost id
props.put("bootstrap.servers", "localhost:9092");

// Set acknowledgements for producer requests using 'acks' property.
props.put("acks", "all");

// If the request fails, the producer can automatically retry using '
    retries' property.
props.put("retries", 0);

// Specify buffer size in config using 'batch.'size property,
props.put("batch.size", 16384);

// Reduce the no of requests less than 0 using 'linger.ms' property.
props.put("linger.ms", 1);

// The buffer.memory controls the total amount of memory available to the
    producer for buffering.
props.put("buffer.memory", 33554432);

props.put("key.serializer",
  "org.apache.kafka.common.serialization.StringSerializer");

props.put("value.serializer",
  "org.apache.kafka.common.serialization.StringSerializer");

Producer<String, String> producer = new KafkaProducer
  <String, String>(props);

for(int i = 0; i < 10; i++)
  producer.send(new ProducerRecord<String, String>(topicName,
    Integer.toString(i), Integer.toString(i)));
      System.out.println("Message⎵sent⎵successfully");
      producer.close();
}
}
```

In this code, we define the properties for the Kafka producer such as
the Kafka server's address, acknowledgments setting, retries, batch
size, and buffer memory. We also specify the serializer classes for
the key and value. Then we create an instance of KafkaProducer
with properties, create a ProducerRecord, and publish it with the
producer's send() function. After publishing all the messages, we
close the producer with the close() function.

Remember that by default the producer doesn't know what type of value you're going to send. It could be a string, integer, or any other object. To convert these types of values into bytes, you have to use a Serializer.

2.8   What is a Kafka consumer?

A Kafka Consumer is a client or an application that consumes records from Kafka clusters. The Kafka Consumer API allows applications to read streams of data from topics in the Kafka cluster.

Kafka uses the 'pull' model to handle large amount of real-time message processing. Consumers send requests to Brokers at regular intervals to retrieve data.

Here's a simple example of a Java Kafka Consumer:

```
import org.apache.kafka.clients.consumer.ConsumerRecord;
import org.apache.kafka.clients.consumer.ConsumerRecords;
import org.apache.kafka.clients.consumer.KafkaConsumer;

import java.util.Arrays;
import java.util.Properties;

public class ExampleConsumer {

    public static void main(String[] args) {

        String topicName = "SampleTopic";
        String groupId = "SampleGroup";

        Properties properties = new Properties();
        properties.put("bootstrap.servers", "localhost:9092");
        properties.put("group.id", groupId);
        properties.put("key.deserializer", "org.apache.kafka.common.
            serialization.StringDeserializer");
        properties.put("value.deserializer", "org.apache.kafka.common.
            serialization.StringDeserializer");

        KafkaConsumer<String, String> consumer = new KafkaConsumer<>(properties
            );
        consumer.subscribe(Arrays.asList(topicName));

        try {
            while (true) {
                ConsumerRecords<String, String> records = consumer.poll(100);
                for (ConsumerRecord<String, String> record : records)
                    System.out.println("Topic:␣" + record.topic() +
                            ",␣Partition:␣" + record.partition() +
```

```
                              ",␣Offset:␣" + record.offset() +
                              ",␣Key:␣" + record.key() +
                              ",␣Value:␣" + record.value());
            }
        } finally {
            consumer.close();
        }
    }
}
```

In this example, we first construct a KafkaConsumer object by specifying some configuration properties. Then we subscribe to a specific topic by calling the 'subscribe()' method. In the loop, we continuously poll new records from the Kafka topic with the 'poll()' method and print the record details. It's important to close the consumer finally to release all the resources.

2.9   What role does ZooKeeper play in a Kafka environment?

ZooKeeper is an integral part of a Kafka environment as it performs various roles that ensure the smooth functioning of a Kafka cluster. The key roles ZooKeeper plays in a Kafka environment include:

1. **Topic Management**: ZooKeeper handles all the topic related functionalities, like topic creation, configuration update, delete, and partition count increment, etc. All topic-related information is stored in ZooKeeper.

2. **Controller Election**: In a Kafka cluster, one of the brokers serves as the controller, which is responsible for managing the states of partitions and replicas. ZooKeeper helps in electing this controller. If a controller crashes, ZooKeeper helps in electing a new one.

3. **Membership Management**: ZooKeeper identifies new broker joining the cluster and keeps track of brokers that are leaving. Effectively, ZooKeeper manages broker presence in the cluster.

4. **Configuration Management**: ZooKeeper is the central repository for all Kafka configuration files. These configurations can be changed in ZooKeeper and will then be propagated to all the brokers.

5. **Synchronization**: ZooKeeper helps in maintaining the broker synchronization process in a Kafka environment.

6. **Message Offset Maintenance**: Finally, ZooKeeper stores the offset of messages consumed in each topic/partition so that, in the event of any system failure, data recovery would be possible.

In short, ZooKeeper helps to ensure that Kafka brokers function correctly and supports failover handling in the event of broker failure. Without ZooKeeper, maintaining the Kafka cluster's coordination would be a difficult task.

Note: Starting from Kafka version 2.8.0, Kafka can also run without ZooKeeper (KRaft mode or KRaft (Kafka Raft metadata) mode), which means ZooKeeper dependency is going to be removed from future Kafka versions.

2.10   What is a consumer group?

A consumer group in Apache Kafka is a group of consumers, identified by a unique string. The main advantage of using a consumer group is that it allows a pool of consumers to divide the processing of data over the topics they are subscribed to. In other words, they are a way of allowing a pool of machines to read from a list of Topics in parallel.

Here is how it works:

1. When a consumer in a group reads a message from a topic, that message is exclusively read by that consumer within that group.

2. Each consumer in a group is assigned a set of partitions from the topic it is subscribed to, therefore using a consumer group allows for

parallel processing.

3. Also, when a new consumer is added into the group, it will start
consuming from a topic partition which was previously consumed
by another consumer. Similarly, if a consumer crashes or if it is
shutdown, then it's partitions will be re-assigned to another consumer
in the same group.

An example of consumer group when consuming from a topic:

```
Properties props = new Properties();
props.put("bootstrap.servers", "localhost:9092");
props.put("group.id", "test"); //this sets the consumer group
props.put("enable.auto.commit", "true");
props.put("auto.commit.interval.ms", "1000");
props.put("key.deserializer", "org.apache.kafka.common.serialization.
     StringDeserializer");
props.put("value.deserializer", "org.apache.kafka.common.serialization.
     StringDeserializer");
KafkaConsumer<String, String> consumer = new KafkaConsumer<>(props);
consumer.subscribe(Arrays.asList("foo", "bar"));
```

In the example above, the consumer is part of the 'test' consumer
group. Because it subscribes to 'foo' and 'bar', the messages from
those topics will be split between the consumers in 'test' group allowing for parallel processing.

2.11   How does Kafka handle scalability?

Apache Kafka is well-known for its high scalability, which enables it to
handle voluminous data and high-speed data inflows. This scalability
is achieved through Kafka's distributed system fundamentals. Here
are the main ways in which Kafka supports scalability:

1. **Partitioning**: Kafka topics are divided into partitions. This
lets Kafka support a big amount of data because each partition can be
placed on a separate server. Moreover, partitions facilitate parallelism
because each Kafka broker can handle data and requests concurrently.

Example: Let's say we have Topic1 with 4 partitions (P1, P2, P3,

P4). These partitions can be hosted on different Kafka brokers (K1, K2, K3, K4), allowing Kafka to handle a large amount of data.

2. **Replication**: Kafka's replication feature offers high availability and fault tolerance. Each partition can be replicated across a configurable number of brokers, meaning if one broker goes down, another can serve the data.

Example: Assuming we have a Kafka cluster with 3 brokers (K1, K2, K3), and we create a topic Topic1 with replication factor 3. Each message produce to this topic will be stored on all three brokers.

3. **Consumer groups**: In Kafka, consumers can read data in parallel by forming a group and dividing the topic partitions among themselves. This boosts Kafka's ability to scale by having multiple consumers reading from a topic at the same time.

Example: Let's assume we have 3 consumers (C1, C2, C3) in consumer group and a topic Topic1 with 3 partitions (P1, P2, P3). Each consumer could be reading from a different partition, which allows for parallel processing.

4. **Horizontal scalability**: Kafka offers the ability to scale out (i.e., increase the number of nodes) to handle larger system loads. By adding more nodes into the Kafka cluster, you can distribute the load among more machines.

Scalability can be tweaked to fit specific needs, and the Kafka architecture allows fine-grained control over these features to strike a balance between data consistency, availability, and network latency.

2.12 What is the difference between a Kafka topic and partition?

A Kafka topic and a Kafka partition are two main components in the architecture of Kafka. They have different purposes and functionalities in the Kafka.

A Kafka topic is a category or a stream name to which the records
are published. Think of it as a logical channel inside Kafka cluster
through which your messages flow. Producers send messages to topics and consumers read messages from topics. Topics are split into
partitions for better parallelism and performance.

Here is how you create a topic:

```
kafka-topics.sh --create --zookeeper localhost:2181 --replication-factor 1 --
    partitions 1 --topic my_topic
```

On the other hand, a Kafka partition is the way by which Kafka
provides redundancy and scalability. Each topic is split into one or
more partitions. These partitions allow you to parallelize a topic
by splitting the data in a particular topic across multiple brokers —
each partition can be placed on a separate machine to allow multiple
consumers to read from a topic in parallel. Producers and consumers
are evenly distributed over partitions.

Here is an example of two topics with multiple partitions:

```
Topic-1            Topic-2
+--------------+ +--------------+
| partition 1 | | partition 1 |
+--------------+ +--------------+
| partition 2 | | partition 2 |
+--------------+ +--------------+
| partition 3 | | partition 3 |
+--------------+ +--------------+
```

In summary, a Kafka Topic is a stream of records. A Kafka Partition
is a part of the Topic which holds a set of these records. Each partition is an ordered, immutable sequence of records that is continually
appended to. They ensure the messages in a topic are distributed
across various nodes in the Kafka cluster, providing high availability
and fault tolerance.

2.13   What is the role of a Kafka broker?

A Kafka broker is a server in Kafka that runs in a Kafka cluster. It holds on to the published messages (also called records) and communicates with producers and consumers.

Here are some of its roles:

1. Receiving Records from Producers: Producers send records to the Kafka broker, which the broker then stores and makes available to consumers. For example, in Java, this may look like this:

```
Properties props = new Properties();
props.put("bootstrap.servers", "localhost:9092");
props.put("key.serializer", "org.apache.kafka.common.serialization.
    StringSerializer");
props.put("value.serializer", "org.apache.kafka.common.serialization.
    StringSerializer");
Producer<String, String> producer = new KafkaProducer<>(props);
ProducerRecord<String, String> record = new ProducerRecord<>("testTopic", "
    value");
producer.send(record);
producer.close();
```

Here 'localhost:9092' refers to the broker. 'testTopic' is the topic to which the record is sent. The broker receives this record and stores it.

2. Serving Records to Consumers: When a consumer wants to consume messages from a topic, it communicates with the Kafka broker. The broker will serve the messages stored in the topic to the consumer. For example,

```
Properties props = new Properties();
props.put("bootstrap.servers", "localhost:9092");
props.put("group.id", "testGroup");
props.put("key.deserializer", "org.apache.kafka.common.serialization.
    StringDeserializer");
props.put("value.deserializer", "org.apache.kafka.common.serialization.
    StringDeserializer");
KafkaConsumer<String, String> consumer = new KafkaConsumer<String, String>(
    props);
consumer.subscribe(Arrays.asList("testTopic"));
while (true) {
  ConsumerRecords<String, String> records = consumer.poll(Duration.ofMillis
      (100));
  for (ConsumerRecord<String, String> record : records)
```

```
    System.out.println(record.value());
}
```

Here, the consumer connects to the broker at 'localhost:9092' and consumes records from the topic 'testTopic'.

3. Participating in Apache Kafka's Distributed Coordination: Kafka brokers also participate in Kafka's distributed coordination. For example, in a Kafka cluster, one of the brokers serves as the controller broker, which is responsible for managing the states of partitions and replicas and for performing administrative tasks like reassigning partitions.

4. Handling Failures: Kafka brokers handle failures and provide data replication to ensure that messages are not lost. If a broker goes down, another broker can serve the data. So, brokers play a significant role in Apache Kafka's fault-tolerance and replication mechanism.

5. Balancing Load: Brokers help in load balancing. Kafka assigns the partitions of a topic across the Kafka brokers in a distributed set-up.

In summary, the Kafka broker is a crucial component that makes the queuing, storage, and transfer of records possible in a Kafka ecosystem. It is responsible for maintaining the records, serving them to consumers, participating in Kafka's distributed coordination, and handling failures and load balancing.

2.14 What is the difference between at-least-once and at-most-once delivery semantics?

At-least-once and at-most-once are two types of delivery semantics in Apache Kafka that specifies when and how messages are sent and acknowledged between producers and consumers.

1. At-least-once:

In at-least-once delivery semantics, messages are guaranteed to be delivered to the broker at least once. In this case, there is no data loss but there might be data duplication. This happens because if a producer sends a message but didn't get an acknowledgment from the broker, it will try to resend the message. The broker might receive the same message more than once and hence the data duplication.

A pseudo code example is shown below:

```
while(true) {
  try {
    producer.send(message);
    break;
  } catch (Exception e) {
    continue;
  }
}
```

Here, the producer will continue trying to send the message until it succeeds.

2. At-most-once:

On contrary, the at-most-once semantics ensures that the messages are either delivered once or not delivered at all i.e., there might be data loss but there will be no data duplication. This is because if a producer sends a data and doesn't hear back from the broker, it will simply assume the data has been processed and it won't resend it.

A pseudo code example is shown below:

```
try {
  producer.send(message);
} catch (Exception e) {
  // ignore and continue
}
```

Here, if the message is not sent on the first attempt, it will not be resent.

In summary:

- At-least-once: Guaranteed delivery, potential for duplicates.

- At-most-once: Potential data loss, but no duplicates.

Choosing between the two would often depend on the use-case or the
type of data,

- If data-loss is a bigger concern, one would choose at-least-once semantics.

- If data duplication can lead to issues (for example financial transactions),
one would prefer to use at-most-once semantics.

2.15   What is Kafka Streams?

Kafka Streams is a client-side library for building applications and
microservices whose data is passed and stored in Kafka. It provides
a high-level Stream DSL (Domain Specific Language) as well as a
low-level Processor API to define stream processing applications.

Unlike other stream processing frameworks, Kafka Streams provides
local storage which allows for stateful stream operations such as joining or windowing.

Kafka Streams combines simplicity with problem-solving power in the
places where you need it the most for microservices development. It
has a lightweight deployment model. You can package and publish
your application into various platforms like Docker, Kubernetes, EC2,
etc., and it does not require any special stream processing cluster.

Kafka Streams apps can be run on machine(s), container(s), virtual
machine(s), or cloud as per the requirements. Below is the example
of Kafka Streams application.

```
import org.apache.kafka.common.serialization.Serdes;
import org.apache.kafka.streams.KafkaStreams;
import org.apache.kafka.streams.StreamsBuilder;
import org.apache.kafka.streams.StreamsConfig;
import org.apache.kafka.streams.kstream.KStream;

import java.util.Properties;

public class StreamApplication {
```

```
public static void main(String[] args){

    Properties props = new Properties();
    props.put(StreamsConfig.APPLICATION_ID_CONFIG, "stream-application");
    props.put(StreamsConfig.BOOTSTRAP_SERVERS_CONFIG, "localhost:9092");
    props.put(StreamsConfig.DEFAULT_KEY_SERDE_CLASS_CONFIG, Serdes.String()
        .getClass());
    props.put(StreamsConfig.DEFAULT_VALUE_SERDE_CLASS_CONFIG, Serdes.String
        ().getClass());

    StreamsBuilder builder = new StreamsBuilder();
    KStream<String, String> textLines = builder.stream("input-topic");
    textLines.mapValues(textLine -> textLine.toLowerCase());
    textLines.to("output-topic");

    KafkaStreams streams = new KafkaStreams(builder.build(), props);
    streams.start();
    }
}
```

In the above example, we first set the required properties for the
streams configuration. Then, the 'StreamsBuilder' is used to create an instance of KStream from an input topic 'input-topic'. The
'mapValues' operation converts each line of text into its lowercase
equivalent. Lastly, the processed messages are sent to the 'output-
topic'.

2.16   What is Kafka Connect?

Apache Kafka Connect is a framework used for connecting Apache
Kafka with external systems such as databases, key-value stores,
search indexes, and file systems. Kafka Connect enables scalable
and reliable streaming of data between Apache Kafka and other data
systems.

It's an API for moving large collections of data into and out of Apache
Kafka, and is especially useful for offloading the effort of reading,
writing, and managing offset for events.

The framework provides a standard service using Kafka to share data
between producers and consumers.

Kafka Connect architecture consists of two main parts:

1. **Source Connectors**: These components import data from external systems into Kafka. For example, you could use a source connector to read data from a database, convert each row to a Kafka record, and publish it to a Kafka topic.

2. **Sink Connectors**: These components export data from Kafka into external systems. For example, a sink connector could consume records from a Kafka topic and write them into a database.

There are several pre-built connectors available such as JDBC connector, Elasticsearch connector, Hadoop/HDFS connector, etc., but you can also build your own custom connectors if needed.

Here is an example for starting a connector:

```
curl -X POST -H "Content-Type:␣application/json" --data '{
"name":␣"my-connector",
"config":␣{
␣␣␣␣"connector.class":␣"com.mycompany.MyConnector",
␣␣␣␣"tasks.max":␣"10",
␣␣␣␣"topics":␣"my-topic",
␣␣␣␣"key.converter":␣"org.apache.kafka.connect.storage.StringConverter",
␣␣␣␣"value.converter":␣"org.apache.kafka.connect.storage.StringConverter",
␣␣␣␣"key.converter.schemas.enable":␣"false",
␣␣␣␣"value.converter.schemas.enable":␣"false",
␣␣␣␣"confluent.topic.bootstrap.servers":␣"localhost:9092",
␣␣␣␣"confluent.topic.replication.factor":␣"1"
}}' http://localhost:8083/connectors
```

This is a RESTful command that creates a new connector named "my-connector" running the class "MyConnector". The connector is set up to run ten tasks across the Connect cluster and consume from the specified topic. The converters specified interpret the keys and values of records as Strings.

2.17 How can you secure Kafka?

Securing Kafka involves implementing several measures either individually or in combination depending on the requirements. These measures aim to ensure only authorized persons are granted access, communications are confidential and data integrity remains uncompromised. Below are detailed steps to secure Kafka:

1. **Authentication**: This is the first level of security and involves
validating the identities of clients trying to communicate with Kafka.
For authentication, Kafka uses SSL or SASL.

a. SSL: SSL can be used for both encryption and client authentication.

```
listeners=SSL://:9093
ssl.keystore.location=/var/private/ssl/kafka.server.keystore.jks
ssl.keystore.password=test1234
ssl.key.password=test1234
ssl.truststore.location=/var/private/ssl/kafka.server.truststore.jks
ssl.truststore.password=test1234
ssl.client.auth=required
```

b. SASL: SASL covers a wide range of authentication mechanisms like GSSAPI(Kerberos), PLAIN, SCRAM etc.

```
listeners=SASL_PLAINTEXT://:9092
sasl.mechanism.inter.broker.protocol=GSSAPI
sasl.kerberos.service.name=kafka
sasl.enabled.mechanisms=GSSAPI
```

2. **Authorization**: After authenticating a client, it is equally
important to determine the level of access granted. Apache Kafka
uses Apache ZooKeeper to maintain and manage its ACLs (Access
Control Lists). These ACLs help in identifying and authorizing or
denying various requests from clients.

```
kafka-acls --authorizer kafka.security.auth.SimpleAclAuthorizer --authorizer
    -properties zookeeper.connect=localhost:2181 --add --allow-principal
    User:Bob --operation Write --topic test-topic
```

3. **Encryption**: To ensure the confidentiality of data being trans-
ferred over network, encryption is essential. Apache Kafka supports
TLS/SSL to provide this feature. The configurations above can also
enable encryption and decryption data for transmission.

4. **Network Isolation**: This can be achieved using Kafka's inbuilt
firewall. More importantly, Kafka allows designing client connections
in such a way that data-intensive traffic and administrative traffic can
be separated.

5. **Quotas**: In order to prevent certain clients from choking up network resources and affecting other clients, Kafka allows setting up quotas.

6. **Auditing**: Kafka doesn't support in-built auditing capabilities. However, it provides necessary details in the form of logs, which can be captured and transformed into meaningful data.

It's also good to keep Kafka brokers updated to the latest stable version containing all the latest security patches.

2.18   What are some use cases for Kafka?

Apache Kafka is a distributed streaming platform designed to handle real-time data feeds. It's a popular choice for most big data, streaming, or data analytics applications because of its robustness and capabilities. Here are some of the use cases:

1. **Messaging**: Kafka works well as a replacement for traditional messaging systems because it is faster and can handle higher volume. It is designed to allow a single cluster to serve as the central data backbone for a large organization.

2. **Website activity tracking**: An activity can be anything like a page view, a search, a click, etc. These activities can be processed and analysed real-time to generate immediate insights for businesses.

3. **Log aggregation**: Logging across multiple services is a classic problem for big distributed systems. Kafka helps to collect log data from multiple services and make it available in a standard format to multiple consumers. It allows for centralized data feeds.

4. **Stream processing**: With the help of Kafka streams, one can easily transform the data from one topic to another in real time. For example, aggregating user events from multiple topics to a single summary topic.

5. **Event sourcing**: Event sourcing is a style of application design where state changes are logged as a time-ordered sequence of records. Kafka, with its storage layer, can allow an application to store this sequence, so it can be used for everything from reconstructing past states to debugging.

6. **Metrics and Monitoring**: Kafka can be used to collect stats from distributed applications and produce centralized feeds of operational data.

7. **Integration with Spark and Flink**: Kafka can plug into Apache Spark and Apache Flink for real-time analysis and rendering of streaming data.

Here is a code snippet to show how Apache Kafka is used for messaging:

```
// Create producer
Properties props = new Properties();
props.put("bootstrap.servers", "localhost:9092");
props.put("key.serializer","org.apache.kafka.common.serialization.
    StringSerializer");
props.put("value.serializer", "org.apache.kafka.common.serialization.
    StringSerializer");

Producer<String, String> producer = new KafkaProducer<>(props);

// send message
ProducerRecord<String, String> record = new ProducerRecord<>("test", "key", "
    value");
producer.send(record);
producer.close();
```

In the above code, we are creating a producer to send messages with a string key and string value to the topic "test" on the local machine.

2.19   How is data retention managed in Kafka?

Data in Kafka is retained in a distributed, partitioned, and replicated commit log service. This log is divided into partitions for better management. All these partitions are ordered, and each one of them is assigned a unique sequential ID number known as the offset.

Data retention in Kafka is managed in two ways:

1. **Time-based Retention:** Kafka has a configuration parameter 'log.retention.hours' (default value is 168 hours i.e., one week). After this time elapses, the log segments are eligible for deletion. This time frame can be customized as per requirements.

```
# Log retention time in hours
log.retention.hours=168
```

2. **Size-based Retention:** Kafka also allows retaining logs based on size. It has a parameter 'log.retention.bytes'. When the size of the log segments exceeds this size, segments are eligible for deletion.

```
# The maximum size of a log segment file. When this size is reached a new log
      segment will be created.
log.segment.bytes=1073741824
```

However, one key thing to note is that data is not immediately deleted when it crosses retention hours or size. Kafka has a background thread that scans log folders periodically (every hour by default) and deletes old log segments.

Also, the deletion policy is set to the log cleanup policy for each topic. If a topic's setting is to "delete" (default), Kafka will delete the old log segment when either retention.ms or retention.bytes is exceeded.

```
# The default cleanup policy for segments beyond the retention window
log.cleanup.policy=delete
```

Another policy "compact" will enable log compaction on the topic i.e., Kafka will ensure that for every key, there is at least one message preserved in the log in the topic.

```
# The default cleanup policy for segments beyond the retention window
log.cleanup.policy=compact
```

Remember though, Kafka guarantees to preserve all messages for the minimum of the retention period set, even if they are consumed.

2.20   What is the significance of the offset in Kafka?

Kafka maintains a numerical offset for each record in a partition. This offset acts as a unique identifier of a record within that partition and denotes the sequence of the record within the partition.

In essence, the offset signifies the position of a consumer in the partition at any given point in time. For example, if we have a consumer at offset 5, this means that the consumer has consumed records up to that point and will next consume the record with offset 6.

The Kafka cluster durably persists all published records—whether or not they have been consumed—using a configurable retention period. For example, if the retention policy is set to two days, then for the two day period after a record is published, it is available for consumption, after which it can be discarded to free up space.

An important point to note about Kafka is that the consumers control the position of the offset. Thus, Kafka has the ability to support a large number of consumers and retains large amounts of data with very little overhead.

We can say that offset in Kafka is maintained per partition basis, not on topic basis.

Java Example:

Here is a simple way how the offset could be managed in Kafka Consumer using Java API:

```
public class KafkaConsumerWithManualOffset {
    private static final String TOPIC_NAME = "testTopic";
    private static final String GROUP_ID = "testGroup";
    private static final String BOOTSTRAP_SERVERS = "localhost:9092";

    public static void main(String[] args) {
        Properties config = new Properties();
        config.put(ConsumerConfig.BOOTSTRAP_SERVERS_CONFIG, BOOTSTRAP_SERVERS);
        config.put(ConsumerConfig.GROUP_ID_CONFIG, GROUP_ID);
        config.put(ConsumerConfig.KEY_DESERIALIZER_CLASS_CONFIG, "org.apache.
            kafka.common.serialization.StringDeserializer");
```

```
config.put(ConsumerConfig.VALUE_DESERIALIZER_CLASS_CONFIG, "org.apache.
    kafka.common.serialization.StringDeserializer");
config.put(ConsumerConfig.ENABLE_AUTO_COMMIT_CONFIG, false);

KafkaConsumer<String, String> consumer = new KafkaConsumer<>(config);
TopicPartition partition0 = new TopicPartition(TOPIC_NAME, 0);
consumer.assign(Arrays.asList(partition0));

while (true) {
    ConsumerRecords<String, String> records = consumer.poll(Duration.
        ofMillis(100));
    for (ConsumerRecord<String, String> record : records) {
        System.out.println(String.format("Topic:␣%s,␣Partition:␣%s,␣
            Offset:␣%s,␣Key:␣%s,␣Value:␣%s",
            record.topic(), record.partition(), record.offset(), record.
                key(), record.value()));
    }
    consumer.commitAsync();
  }
 }
}
```

In this code snippet, we create a KafkaConsumer, then we disable the auto-commit of offsets by setting enable.auto.commit to false. Instead, we manually commit the offsets after processing each record from the TopicPartition, thus controlling the offset positions.

Chapter 3

Intermediate

3.1 How does Kafka ensure data durability?

Apache Kafka ensures data durability through a combination of techniques like replication, persistence, and write-ahead logs (WAL).

1. **Replication**: Kafka replicates each message across multiple broker instances (usually three). The number of replicas is configurable to allow for geographical distribution and increasing levels of protection. Kafka ensures that as long as a single replica survives, no data is lost by maintaining the ISR (In-Sync Replica) set which includes all the active replicas that are caught-up with the leader. To ensure durability in case of a broker failure, it is crucial that at least one in-sync replica is alive when the broker goes down. This replica will assume the role of the leader and continue operation.

```
# To configure replication factor
replication.factor=3
```

2. **Persistence**: Kafka maintains message durability by persisting

all the message data onto the disk. Kafka's storage layout is simple
and allows message persistence through the file system, resulting in
reduced latency for data access.

```
# Kafka stores logs (message data) in /tmp/kafka-logs/ directory
log.dirs=/tmp/kafka-logs/
```

3. **Write-ahead logs (WAL)**: Lastly, Kafka utilizes the write-
ahead logs (WAL) which is also a primary durability feature. When
a producer sends a message to Kafka, the broker writes the message
to its log but doesn't immediately confirm the message has been published to the consumer. Instead, a page-cache mechanism is used in
Kafka. So what happens is data will be written to the page cache,
and the OS will be responsible for flushing data to disk from time to
time, which increases Kafka's throughput.

In summary, the combination of these three features provides Kafka
durability by allowing it to survive single or multiple node failures,
ensuring no message loss, and serving massive reads and writes. Contrast to some traditional message systems which use a level of caching
to improve the message flow, thus could potentially lose the data if a
catastrophic failure occurs.

3.2   Explain the difference between a leader and a follower partition in Kafka.

Apache Kafka is based on the distributed architecture, meaning it
distributes the load of managing the data across different servers.
In Kafka, data is stored in Topics. Topics consist of one or more
Partitions, and these Partitions are distributed across different servers
(Kafka brokers) to balance the load. Each Partition has one Leader
and zero or more Followers.

Leader Partition: The leader partition manages all read and
write requests for the partition. When a producer publishes a message to a topic, it actually sends it to the leader partition of the topic.

Similarly, when consumers wish to read messages, they also connect to the leader partition.

Follower Partition: These are the replicated partitions that exist on other Kafka brokers. The follower partitions passively replicate the leader partition. The primary purpose is for failover handling. If the leader fails, one of the follower partitions will become the new leader.

The main difference between them lies in their activities: 1. The Leader is active and handles all requests for a partition, whereas the follower is passive and just replicates the data of the leader. 2. In case of a leader failure, one of the followers will become the new leader.

Here is a simple example of a Kafka Cluster consisting of 3 brokers (B1, B2, and B3), with a Topic T which consists of 3 partitions (P1, P2, and P3):

```
B1(Broker1) - P1(Leader),   P2(Follower), P3(Follower)
B2(Broker2) - P1(Follower), P2(Leader),   P3(Follower)
B3(Broker3) - P1(Follower), P2(Follower), P3(Leader)
```

In this case, B1 is the leader for partition P1 and followers are on B2 and B3. Similarly for P2 and P3. If B1 crashes, then for partition P1, either B2 or B3 will become the leader (based on Kafka's leader election process).

3.3 How does Kafka handle failover for its brokers?

In Kafka, broker failover is mainly handled by the concept of replication, which ensures data durability and high availability. The fundamental idea behind replication is to duplicate the data across multiple nodes, which ensures that data is not lost even if one of the nodes (broker) fails.

Replication in Kafka is achieved by maintaining multiple copies of each topic partition across different brokers. One of these brokers is designated as the leader, and the rest of them serve as followers. The leader handles all the read and write requests for the partition, while the followers passively replicate the leader's data. When the leader fails, one of the followers will automatically be elected as the new leader.

This process is managed by another component of Kafka known as Zookeeper. Zookeeper performs broker leader election when a failure occurs. When a broker goes offline, Zookeeper will notice the broker's absence and triggers a re-election of the leader for all partitions that were led by the failed broker.

Replication factor is critical in a Kafka deployment as it decides the number of copies of the data that are maintained. A replication factor of 3, for example, means that each topic partition data is duplicated across three brokers.

Below shows how Kafka replica placement strategy handles failover:

```
public class DefaultReplicaPlacementStrategy implements
    ReplicaPlacementStrategy {

    @Override
    public Map<TopicPartition, List<Integer>> placeReplicas(Map<Integer, List<
        Integer>> rackToBrokerMap,
                                        int replicationFactor, Set<
                                            String> topics,
                                        Map<String,
                                            InternalTopicConfig>
                                            topicConfigs) {
        double rackSpread = 100.0 * rackToBrokerMap.size() / replicationFactor;
        if (rackSpread < MIN_RACK_SPREAD_PERCENT) {
            log.warn("The number of racks {} is less than total brokers count
                {} multiplied by 'min.insync.replicas' {}. " +
                    "This will hurt availability of your Kafka cluster",
                    rackToBrokerMap.size(), replicationFactor, rackSpread);
        }
        Map<TopicPartition, List<Integer>> replicaAssignment = new HashMap<>();
        for (String topic : topics) {
            int numPartitions = topicConfigs.get(topic).numberOfPartitions();
            for (int partition = 0; partition < numPartitions; partition++) {
                ArrayList<Integer> brokers = selectBrokers(rackToBrokerMap,
                    replicationFactor);
                replicaAssignment.put(new TopicPartition(topic, partition),
                    brokers);
            }
        }
        return replicaAssignment;
    }
```

}

It's crucial to remember that a higher replication factor can increase the reliability and fault tolerance, but at the same time, it would also increase the cost as more storage and network bandwidth are needed.

Kafka also supports unclean leader election, where a follower that didn't fully sync with the leader can also be elected as the leader. This feature can significantly decrease the downtime, but it may lead to data loss. Therefore, you should turn it on based on your own needs.

3.4 What is the role of the ISR (In-Sync Replicas) in Kafka?

In Apache Kafka, ISR stands for In-Sync Replicas. In a Kafka cluster, each individual partition of a topic has one leader and zero or more followers. The leader handles all reads and writes for the partition, and the followers passively replicate the leader. If the followers keep pace with the leader, they are considered "in-sync". Kafka maintains a dynamically updated set of in-sync replicas (ISRs) for every partition. The main purpose of ISR is to prevent data loss.

Kafka only completes a producer's write once the data has been successfully copied on all in-sync replicas. This means once a message is written to the partition, it's written to the leader and all the in-sync follower replicas. This strategy guarantees that any message that has been acknowledged by the broker can be successfully served even if the leader fails. If the leader fails, one of the followers will become the new leader.

The key properties of ISR dictated by Kafka configurations are:

- 'min.insync.replicas' decides the minimum number of insync replicas that should exist for the produce request to be successful.

- 'replica.lag.time.max.ms' decides the maximum allowed time for a replica to be out of sync. If it's out of sync for longer than this period, it will be removed from ISR.

Kafka example with ISR:

Suppose there are 3 replicas and the ISR has all the three in place: [1,2,3]. Now, if the third replica doesn't get updated in time with the leader it gets removed from the ISR and our ISR becomes [1,2]. The client can get this updated ISR to know the state of the Kafka cluster. Only if these In-sync replicas acknowledge the write, a success message is sent to the producer.

Even with all of these, if at any time number of insync replicas fail to meet the 'min.insync.replicas' setting, the producer will raise a 'NotE-noughReplicasException', which is how Kafka ensures durability of messages. The ISR list plays an essential role to ensure reliability and durability in Kafka.

3.5   Describe the write and read operations in Kafka with respect to the leader and follower partitions.

In Kafka, data is stored in topics which are split into different partitions. A partition can be replicated across multiple servers for fault-tolerance, which ensures that data is still available if a server fails. Each partition has one server acting as the "leader", and zero or more servers acting as "followers".

Write Operations: All producers send data to the leader and the data is written onto the leader first. The leader records all changes to its partitions in a data structure called the "write-ahead-log". The write operation is considered successful after the data is stored in the leader's memory, regardless of it being replicated to other brokers.

However, Kafka also allows configuring the acknowledgements ('acks') to control how data is written to ensure the durability of messages. The three possible configuration values are:

* 'acks=0': This means the producer does not wait for any acknowledgment from the broker that it has received the data. This option provides the most potential throughput but the least durability.

* 'acks=1': This means the producer waits for acknowledgment from the broker that the leader has received the data. This option provides better durability as the producer suffers a performance hit for the round-trip it takes to get broker acknowledgment.

* 'acks=all' or 'acks=-1': This means the producer waits for acknowledgment from "all" in-sync replicas (ISRs). If any of the in-sync replicas goes out of sync, a producer set to 'acks=all' will receive an exception.

After the leader receives the record, the record is then appended in the followers asynchronously. Replicas that are in sync are part of the ISR (in-sync replicas) list.

Read Operations: Only the leader serves client consumers for all read and write requests. The followers consume messages from the leader just like a normal Kafka consumer.

Here is a pseudocode for the Kafka producer and consumer:

```
// producer
Properties props = new Properties();
props.put("bootstrap.servers", "localhost:9092");
props.put("acks", "all");
Producer<String, String> producer = new KafkaProducer<>(props);

for(int i = 0; i < 100; i++)
    producer.send(new ProducerRecord<String, String>("my-topic", Integer.
        toString(i), Integer.toString(i)));

producer.close();

// consumer
Properties props = new Properties();
props.put("bootstrap.servers", "localhost:9092");
props.put("group.id", "test");
props.put("auto.offset.reset", "earliest");
Consumer<String, String> consumer = new KafkaConsumer<>(props);
```

```
consumer.subscribe(Arrays.asList("my-topic"));

while (true) {
    ConsumerRecords<String, String> records = consumer.poll(100);
    for (ConsumerRecord<String, String> record : records)
        System.out.printf("offset␣=␣%d,␣key␣=␣%s,␣value␣=␣%sn", record.offset()
            , record.key(), record.value());
}
```

This model ensures strong durability and fault-tolerance guarantees.
However, the leader does periodic checks to see if the follower is still
in sync. If the follower has not sent any requests in a time window
larger than the 'replica.lag.time.max.ms' (defaults to 10 seconds), the
leader removes it from the ISR list and it no longer receives any data.

Any Kafka-Broker can be elected as the Partition-Leader. The leader
election algorithm is pluggable. By default Kafka uses the 'round-
robin' algorithm. This property is defined by 'auto.leader.rebalance.enable'.
If it is set to true, periodic leader balance checks take place and leaders are reelected, if necessary.

3.6   What is log compaction in Kafka, and why is it useful?

Log compaction is a mechanism in Apache Kafka that gives a per-
key semantics for retaining data. It allows Kafka to retain the largest
offset/last entry for each key in the log for a longer amount of time,
while the old, less relevant data is discarded. This solves the problem
of logs growing indefinitely and causing storage issues.

With normal deletion policies, once data is older than the maximum
retention period (typically seven days), Kafka deletes it irrespective of
the state. This deletion policy is a problem if consumer applications
are offline for extended periods of time. By using log compaction,
Kafka guarantees that it will always retain at least the last known
value for each message key within the log of data for each topic partition.

The compaction process works in the background to clean the log files and retain only the last update made to each message key. Here is how the process works:

1. Log cleaner, the primary actor in log compaction process, scans through the log from the beginning, identifying sections of the log called "segments".

2. It works on each segment, writing all messages to the output, keeping only the last message for each key.

3. It replaces the old segment with the new, compacted segment.

In terms of storage, log compaction provides a more efficient usage by only storing the latest update for each key.

Let's say we have a sequence of messages:

```
Key A, Value X (Offset 0)
Key B, Value Y (Offset 1)
Key A, Value Z (Offset 2)
Key A, Value W (Offset 3)
Key B, Value P (Offset 4)
```

After log compaction, this would be reduced to:

```
Key A, Value W (Offset 3)
Key B, Value P (Offset 4)
```

Here we can see only the latest values for each key are retained, decreasing the size of stored data. This is particularly beneficial in use cases like restoring state after failure or bootstraping a new node, where you're only interested in the current state rather than the full history.

3.7 How do you handle schema evolution in Kafka messages?

Schema evolution in Kafka messages can be handled using Apache Avro, a data serialization system which has excellent support for schema evolution. Apache Avro is integrated with the Confluent Schema Registry that is used with Apache Kafka.

The Schema Registry stores a versioned history of all schemas and allows for the evolution of schemas according to the configured compatibility setting and expanded Avro support. Producers write data with a schema id and consumers read the data and use the id to fetch the schema from the Schema Registry for deserialization.

Here are the four strategies for schema evolution:

1. Backward compatibility: A new schema can be used to read data written in any older schema. A change is backward compatible if a consumer using the update schema can read all data produced with the last schema.

```
{
    "type":"record",
    "name":"Customer",
    "fields":[
        {
            "name":"first_name",
            "type":"string"
        },
    ]
}
```

2. Forward compatibility: A new schema works with data written by any previous schema. A change is forward compatible if a message serialized with a new schema can be read by consumers using the old schema.

3. Full compatibility: A change is fully compatible if it is both forward and backward compatible.

4. None: No compatibility guarantees.

To handle schema evolution:

- Always give default values to new fields.

- Be careful when using enum types because Avro doesn't support adding symbols in enums.

- Never rename fields.

- When evolving a schema, set the compatibility type to 'NONE' if you want to ignore an Avro's default compatibility check and avoid evolution constraints.

Schema evolution is an essential aspect of Kafka. Following these strategies, it would be safer to modify schemas and ensure applications do not break due to incompatible changes.

3.8 What are windowed operations in Kafka Streams?

Windowed operations in Kafka Streams are operations that perform computations on a defined subset of data based on a specific time window.

For instance, one might want to calculate the average of some values, but not on the total stream of data. Instead, you might be interested in calculating this average just over the data of the last five minutes. This is where the windowed operations come in.

There are three types of windows in Kafka Streams:

- Tumbling windows: These are a series of fixed-size, non-overlapping windows.

- Hopping windows: These are also a series of fixed-size windows, but they can be overlapped. This means that a particular record could belong to more than one window.

- Sliding windows: These windows are not fixed and can move freely. They also overlap and usually represent the last N units of time before a certain event.

Here is a simple example code that uses tumbling windows in Kafka
Streams:

```
KTable<Windowed<String>, Long> counts = stream.groupByKey()
  .windowedBy(TimeWindows.of(Duration.ofMinutes(5)))
  .count();
```

In this example, a tumbling window of 5 minutes is created. The
'groupByKey' operation is grouping the records by their keys, and
for each 5-minute window, the 'count' operation will calculate the
number of records. The result is a 'KTable' that contains each unique
key and the count of the records for each 5-minute window.

3.9   How does Kafka ensure exactly-once semantics?

Apache Kafka ensures exactly once semantics through Transactions.

Exactly-once semantics in Kafka is achieved through two major operations:

1) Idempotent Writes: The idea here is that each batch of messages
written to Kafka will be given a sequence number. When Kafka
receives batches from a producer, it will compare the sequence number
with the last sequence number it has seen from the same producer.
If it's not expecting the sequenced batch, the write is rejected as a
duplicate.

For example, if a producer sent batches A, B, C, and D in that order,
each would have a sequence number incremented by 1 (A:1, B:2, C:3,
D:4). If the producer failed after sending batch C, but that batch
somehow takes longer to get to Kafka than batch D,then when the
producer is restarted, it may resend batch C. But because Kafka has
already seen a batch D with a higher sequence number, it will reject
batch C when it arrives.

This is enabled by setting 'enable.idempotence=true' in the producer's configuration.

2) Transactions: Apache Kafka permits applications to write to multiple partitions in a transactional manner. A producer can either complete the entire set of writes successfully or none of them. It ensures atomic writes even when the updates are spread across multiple partitions.

Transactions in Apache Kafka are defined using the methods 'beginTransaction()', 'send()', 'commitTransaction()', 'abortTransaction()' in 'KafkaProducer'. They encompass every kind of operation that deals with Kafka, including sending messages via a producer and consuming messages via a consumer.

Example producer configuration for transactions:

```
testProducerProps = {
  'bootstrap.servers': 'localhost:9092',
  'key.serializer': 'org.apache.kafka.common.serialization.StringSerializer',
  'value.serializer': 'org.apache.kafka.common.serialization.StringSerializer'
  ,
  'transactional.id': 'test-transactional-id'
}

producer = KafkaProducer(**testProducerProps)
producer.init_transactions()

try:
  producer.begin_transaction()
  producer.send('test-topic', key='test-key', value='test-value')
  producer.commit_transaction()
except Exception as e:
  print('Transaction failed', e)
  producer.abort_transaction()
```

To ensure end-to-end exactly-once processing semantics, you also need transactional consumers, which don't fetch messages that are part of open transactions.

The combination of idempotent producers and Kafka's support for transactions ensures exactly-once semantics in Apache Kafka.'

3.10   What is the difference between commitSync and commitAsync in Kafka?

In Apache Kafka, the 'commitSync' and 'commitAsync' functions are used to commit offsets. It helps Kafka to keep track of the records that have already been consumed from a topic and what record will be consumed next. The differences between commitSync and commitAsync are primarily based on reliability and the way these methods provide responses.

* **commitSync**: The 'commitSync' method sends a request to the Kafka cluster to commit the current consumer's offset and waits for the cluster's response before moving ahead. It follows a synchronous way of committing the consumer offset.

If the 'commitSync' method fails, it will retry committing the offset until it succeeds or encounters a non-retriable failure. While this increases the reliability of the offset commit, it raises the possibility that the processing of the records could be blocked if the Kafka cluster becomes unavailable or encounters an error.

Here is an example of commitSync:

```
try {
    consumer.commitSync();
} catch (CommitFailedException e) {
    // logic to handle commit exceptions
}
```

* **commitAsync**: The 'commitAsync' method, on the other hand, behaves in an asynchronous manner. It will send a request to commit the current consumer offset but will not wait for a response from the Kafka cluster. It continues to consume and process the next records.

The 'commitAsync' method does not block the consumer's process hence, it has higher throughput than 'commitSync'. However, it provides less reliability since it does not retry to commit the offset in case of failure. If the commit fails, the 'commitAsync' function will not retry and just throw an exception.

Here is an example of commitAsync:

```
consumer.commitAsync(new OffsetCommitCallback() {
    public void onComplete(Map<TopicPartition, OffsetAndMetadata> offsets,
        Exception e) {
        if (e != null) {
          // logic to handle commit exceptions
        }
}});
```

In essence, 'commitSync' provides higher reliability at the cost of lower throughput, while 'commitAsync' provides higher throughput with less reliability. Which one to use depends on the requirement of your application.

3.11 How does Kafka handle message compression? Which compression types does it support?

Apache Kafka uses message compression as a way to optimize the performance of message-heavy systems. It balances efficient storage and network utilization with CPU usage, depending upon the specific use case.

In Kafka, both the producer and the consumer are aware of the compression algorithm used. This means that compression happens at the producer end before sending the messages, reducing the computational load on the consumer's side.

Producers set the CompressionType attribute in the ProducerConfig to enable message compression. If a batch of messages is compressed in the producer, it will be decompressed in the consumer in a whole batch manner to avoid the costly overhead of decompressing individual messages. Kafka also retains the compressed messages in their batches as long as they live in Kafka, which saves storage space.

As of Kafka version 2.1, Kafka producer supports three types of compression: GZIP, Snappy, and LZ4.

GZIP provides a good compression rate (high compression ratio), but it requires high computational resources. It is a good option if CPU cycles are less of a concern than bandwidth.

Snappy, developed by Google, provides moderate compression with less CPU overhead. It's optimized for high speeds rather than a high compression ratio.

LZ4 is designed to be a fast compression algorithm, providing very high-speed compression and decompression but with lower ratios.

Here is a sample of how to set the compression type in the Kafka Producer configuration:

```
Properties props = new Properties();
props.put("bootstrap.servers", "localhost:9092");
props.put("acks", "all");
props.put("compression.type", "gzip"); // Set compression type to gzip
props.put("key.serializer", "org.apache.kafka.common.serialization.
    StringSerializer");
props.put("value.serializer", "org.apache.kafka.common.serialization.
    StringSerializer");
Producer<String, String> producer = new KafkaProducer<String, String>(props);
```

The type of compression used is use-case specific. For high-speed systems, LZ4 or Snappy might be more appropriate, while for systems where the network is a bottleneck, GZIP may be a better choice.

3.12   Explain the concept of a "consumer lag" in Kafka.

Consumer lag in Apache Kafka is the delay caused by the difference in rate at which the producer is producing data and the rate at which the consumer is consuming data. The term "lag" is generally associated with delays or slowness in a system. Hence, Kafka Consumer Lag is an indicator of the consumer's slowness.

When a Kafka producer produces data, it gets written to a Kafka topic. The data within a topic is divided and stored onto different partitions, where it is then picked up by Kafka consumers. Each consumer within the consumer group keeps track of the offset, which represents the position of the consumer in the topic partition.

The consumer will then read the next message from where the last offset was, increment the offset count and continue this process. In an ideal scenario, the consumer processes the records as soon as the producer produces them. However, if the consumer cannot keep up with the producer, there will be messages in the topic that have been produced but not yet consumed. This lag/difference in processing is referred to as Consumer Lag.

To monitor consumer lag, you can use a tool such as Kafka's command-line utility "kafka-consumer-groups.sh". Here's a simple command to describe the lag of a specific consumer group:

```
kafka-consumer-groups.sh --bootstrap-server kafka_broker:9092 --describe --
    group consumer_group
```

The '–describe' flag will give you a detailed description of the group, including the "current-offset", "log-end-offset", and the resultant "lag". Consumer lag is calculated as the difference between the "log-end-offset" (the offset up to which the producer has written) and the "current-offset" (the offset up to which the consumer has consumed).

Frequent monitoring of consumer lag is crucial in a production environment as a high lag indicates a slower consumer, which may eventually result in data loss or delays in processing, hampering the real-time processing characteristics of Kafka.

3.13   How can you rebalance the partitions among brokers?

Apache Kafka's design allows it to handle failover of brokers in a Kafka cluster or when adding new brokers. This is achieved by re-assigning the topic partitions among all the brokers so that load is equally distributed among them.

A typical Kafka cluster has many topics, each divided into multiple partitions. These partitions are spread over Kafka brokers that form the cluster.

The assignment of the partition to a broker is held by Zookeeper service. When a broker is down or a new broker is added, the distribution of the partitions among the brokers becomes uneven. To bring back the balance, the partitions need to be reassigned.

This can be achieved using Kafka's partition reassignment tool. The steps to use this tool are as follows:

Step 1. Generate a JSON file that defines the new assignments of partitions to brokers. Here is an example JSON file:

```
{
  "partitions": [
    {
      "topic": "my-topic",
      "partition": 0,
      "replicas": [1,2,3]
    },
    {
      "topic": "my-topic",
      "partition": 1,
      "replicas": [2,3,1]
    },
    ...
  ]
}
```

Step 2. Run the command to start the reassignment process.

```
kafka-reassign-partitions --zookeeper localhost:2181 --reassignment-json-file
    my-reassignment.json --execute
```

When running, it stops consumers and producers, reassigns and syncs replicas to the new machines, and then resumes the consumers and producers again.

Step 3. Verify the reassignment process.

```
kafka-reassign-partitions --zookeeper localhost:2181 --reassignment-json-file
    my-reassignment.json --verify
```

This is how you can rebalance partitions among brokers. This process ensures high availability and failover handled by Kafka.

Do note that Kafka's automated replication only moves replicas of existing partitions to the new broker; it does not rebalance other replicas. It is essential to monitor the distribution of load among brokers and reassign partitions when necessary to ensure efficient data processing.

Note that the above commands can result in significant data shifting and should be planned and monitored closely in a production environment. Always ensure you have enough disk capacity and network bandwidth before starting the reassignment.

The new Kafka versions also allow KIP-455, which includes removing replicas in a controlled manner, changing the hours in which a removal can occur, and allowing a removal to be canceled if needed.

3.14 What is the purpose of the ___consumer_offsets topic in Kafka?

The '___consumer_offsets' is a special topic in Apache Kafka used to track the progress of a Kafka Consumer during the data consumption process. Each Kafka consumer within the group maintains its offset, or position, within each partition. This offset information is vital because it allows Kafka to keep track of the messages that have been consumed and those that are yet to be processed.

Whenever a consumer reads a message from a partition, it commits
the offset of messages up to which it has consumed. Kafka then stores
these offsets within the '__consumer_offsets' topic, which implies
that the offset storage is durable and can survive broker restarts.

This mechanism allows Consumers to resume their work from where
they left off in the event of failures or restarts. It's particularly important for ensuring at least once delivery semantics - if a consumer
fails after processing a message but before committing its offset, it
might process the same message again after recovery completes.

If a consumer group id changes, Kafka would not be able to find
the previously committed offset, and the behavior would be as per
'auto.offset.reset' property settings.

Please note that this topic is not meant for direct user interaction. It
should be managed and interacted with via the KafkaConsumer API
calls. You can however inspect it for debugging purposes using the
Kafka-console-consumer, filtering by key to the group id of interest.

```
kafka-console-consumer --bootstrap-server localhost:9092 --topic
    __consumer_offsets --formatter "kafka.coordinator.group.
    GroupMetadataManager$OffsetsMessageFormatter" --from-beginning
```

This command allows you to inspect the offset commit messages,
showing the topic, partition, offset, and timestamp for each commit.

3.15   How does Kafka Connect ensure fault tolerance and scalability?

Apache Kafka Connect is a tool for scalably and reliably streaming
data between Apache Kafka and other data systems in a fault-tolerant
manner. The fault tolerance and scalability of Kafka Connect are
achieved by two main functionalities:

1. **Distributed Mode**: Kafka Connect can run in either standalone mode or distributed mode. In standalone mode, all work is

performed in a single process. In distributed mode, the work is divided among multiple worker processes which might run across multiple machines or server instances. This makes Kafka Connect scalable since adding more machines to the cluster increases the capacity of data that can be processed. Thus, as your system-oriented tasks increase, instead of overloading a single machine, you can add more machines to your Kafka Connect cluster.

2. **Fault-Tolerance**: Kafka Connect uses Kafka to persist the offsets of connectors and tasks (in the 'config', 'status', and 'offsets' topics). This not only means that the progress of data copying is stored, but also that it can be recovered upon failure. If a machine fails, Kafka Connect migrates the entire workload of failed workers to the rest of the running workers in the cluster. In the case that a task fails, Connect will try restarting the task on the same worker, and if it continues to fail, it will cease invoking the faulty task and report an error. Also, because of running in distributed mode, the system is resilient to worker failures. If a worker crashes, the tasks get reassigned to other live workers ensuring no loss of service.

Here is the code on how you can start a worker in distributed mode in JSON format:

```
{
  "name": "connect-cluster",
  "config": {
    "bootstrap.servers": "localhost:9094",
    "group.id": "connect-cluster",
    "offset.storage.topic": "connect-cluster-offsets",
    "offset.storage.replication.factor": "3",
    "status.storage.topic": "connect-cluster-status",
    "status.storage.replication.factor": "3",
    "config.storage.topic": "connect-cluster-configs",
    "config.storage.replication.factor": "3",
    "key.converter": "org.apache.kafka.connect.json.JsonConverter",
    "value.converter": "org.apache.kafka.connect.json.JsonConverter",
    "key.converter.schemas.enable": "true",
    "value.converter.schemas.enable": "true",
  }
}
```

In this configuration:

- 'group.id': This is a unique string that identifies the Connect cluster group this worker belongs to.

- 'offset.storage.topic', 'status.storage.topic', 'config.storage.topic': These topics define where the worker should store connector offsets, status information, and configuration data respectively.

- '*.storage.replication.factor': Kafka replication factor ensures that connector configuration, offset, and status data are highly available and, hence, adds resilience.

These features make Kafka Connect a suitable tool for large-scale and mission-critical applications where data consistency and system resilience are of high importance.

3.16   What are the different types of connectors in Kafka Connect (source vs. sink)?

Kafka Connect is a powerful tool for building real-time data pipelines between Apache Kafka and other data systems. Connectors are the components of Kafka Connect that move data in and out of Apache Kafka.

There are two types of connectors in Kafka Connect: source connectors and sink connectors.

Source Connectors

Source connectors pull data from another system into Kafka. For instance, we could use a source connector for reading log files and generating records to a Kafka topic, or to ingest data from a database.

Here is a basic structure of a source connector config file in JSON format:

```
{
  "name": "source-connector-name",
  "config": {
    "connector.class": "org.apache.kafka.connect.file.
        FileStreamSourceConnector",
    "tasks.max": "1",
```

```
    "file": "/path/to/input/file",
    "topic": "input-topic"
  }
}
```

This configuration file instructs Kafka Connect to start a file source connector that will read data from the specified file and publish it to the specified topic.

Sink Connectors

Sink connectors take data from Kafka and push it into other systems. For example, a sink connector can be used to write data from a Kafka topic into a file or to load data into a database.

Here is an example of a sink connector config file (also in JSON format):

```
{
  "name": "sink-connector-name",
  "config": {
    "connector.class": "org.apache.kafka.connect.file.FileStreamSinkConnector"
,
    "tasks.max": "1",
    "file": "/path/to/output/file",
    "topics": "output-topic"
  }
}
```

This configuration starts a file sink connector that takes data from the specified topic and writes it to the specified output file.

In summary, the type of connector you use will depend on the direction of data flow you require: source connectors for ingesting data into Kafka, and sink connectors for transporting data from Kafka to external systems.

3.17   How do you handle large messages in Kafka?

Handling large messages in Apache Kafka can be quite a challenge given Kafka's scalability and performance design principles. By default, Kafka has a maximum fetch and transmit message size of 1MB for each topic partition. Here are some ways to handle large messages:

1. **Increase the maximum message size**: Increase the maximum message size at the broker and producer by setting 'message.max.bytes' and 'replica.fetch.max.bytes' configs on the broker, and 'max.request.size' on the producer. But note that increasing the message size can cause JVM to pause during garbage collections and increase end-to-end latency.

```
# Broker-Level configs
message.max.bytes=20000000 #<this decides the maximum size of message that the
    broker can receive
replica.fetch.max.bytes=30000000 #<this decides the maximum size of message
    that the broker can replicate

# Producer-level Config
max.request.size=20000000 #< Maximum size of request in bytes
```

2. **Message compression**: Kafka supports compression at the producer and decompression at the consumer. Kafka supports GZIP, LZ4, and Snappy. Producers can choose to send data in compressed format, and Kafka stores it in the format the data was received. This can be set by 'compression.type' parameter at producer level.

```
compression.type=snappy #< this will enable snappy compression on producer
```

3. **Split large messages**: If the messages are too large, consider splitting them into smaller messages. This logic needs to be handled in your producer and consumer. Producers will split the large message into smaller ones, possibly with sequence identifiers for correct ordering, and consumers will reassemble these small messages back into the large message.

4. **Use an External Store**: For extremely large messages, another

option is to store these messages (or message payloads) in an external store like HDFS or S3 and just send the links to these files in Kafka messages.

Remember, it's not only about increasing the message size, but Kafka is also about real-time, low latency processing. Large messages increase the latency of the system, so you must always strike a balance between message size and system constraints.

3.18 What are the potential issues with having too many partitions in a Kafka cluster?

While partitioning in Apache Kafka aids in achieving higher consumer parallelism, having too many partitions in a Kafka cluster can lead to issues, too. The potential issues include:

1. **Increased Latency**: Each request served by a broker has some amount of overhead. Thus, an increase in partitions may lead to an increase in the number of requests, thereby increasing the latency.

If there are more partitions, the broker will need to manage more file descriptors and socket connections. This can put a strain on resources and increase end-to-end latency.

2. **Increased Leader Elections**: With more partitions, there will be more leaders. Therefore, during a broker failure, Zookeeper will need to coordinate more leader elections, which can lead to Zookeeper performance degradation.

3. **Higher Memory Usage**: More partitions mean more memory usage. The reason is that Kafka's controller needs approximately 1KB of heap memory per partition. The JVM may get into out-of-memory exceptions if the controller is not correctly configured with larger heap size when there are a large number of partitions.

4. **Increase in Recovery Time**: The failure recovery process takes more time with an excessive number of partitions. If a Kafka broker goes down, it has to recover each partition one by one, which can take a substantial amount of time if there are many partitions.

5. **Overhead on Consumer Side**: On the consumer side, whether using the high or simple consumer, each consumer connection holds metadata about all its relevant partitions. As partition count goes up, this will increase the amount of metadata the consumer has to hold and may negatively affect consumer performance.

Remember that while determining the number of partitions, care must be taken to strike a balance so that there are enough partitions to achieve higher parallelism and, at the same time, not too many partitions such that it takes a toll on performance.

3.19   Describe the process of setting up SSL authentication for a Kafka cluster.

Setting up SSL for a Kafka cluster involves generating SSL keys and certificates for brokers, creating SSL trust stores, creating and configuring a Kubernetes secret, and configuring SSL for Schema Registry, Kafka Connect, and clients.

Here's a more detailed step-by-step process:

Step 1: Generating SSL keys and certificates for brokers

Firstly, you need to create a private key for each Kafka broker. The key is used to encrypt the data transmitted between the clients and the broker. The following command can be used to generate a private key:

```
keytool -keystore server.keystore.jks -alias localhost -validity 365 -genkey
```

Step 2: Creating SSL truststore

Truststore is used to store public keys and certificates from the CA (Certificate Authority). It is used when the client wants to authenticate the server during the SSL handshake process. You can create a truststore using the following command:

```
keytool -keystore kafka.server.truststore.jks -alias CARoot -import -file ca-
    cert
```

Step 3: Creating and Configuring Kubernetes Secret (if Kafka is running in Kubernetes)

The generated truststore and keystore need to be added to your Kubernetes infrastructure as secrets, which Apache Kafka can access during deployment. You can do this with the following commands:

```
kubectl create secret generic broker-ssl -from-file=./broker-1.keystore.p12 -
    from-file=./broker-1.truststore.jks

kubectl create secret generic client-ssl --from-file=./client.truststore.jks
```

Step 4: Configuring SSL for Schema Registry, Kafka Connect, and Clients

SSL needs to be enabled for Kafka's related services as well. For example, to configure SSL for the Kafka schema registry and Kafka Connect, add these lines to the properties file:

```
ssl.truststore.location=/var/private/ssl/kafka.client.truststore.jks
ssl.truststore.password=test1234
ssl.keystore.location=/var/private/ssl/kafka.client.keystore.jks
ssl.keystore.password=test1234
ssl.key.password=test1234
```

Similarly, the clients (producers and consumers) talking to the Kafka broker also need to use SSL and have their SSL properties set.

Step 5: Enabling SSL in Kafka Brokers

In order for Kafka brokers to accept SSL connections, server.properties file needs to be updated to include SSL protocols, keystore and truststore files. A segment of your updated configuration might look similar to this:

```
listeners=PLAINTEXT://:9092,SSL://:9093
ssl.keystore.location=/var/private/ssl/kafka.server.keystore.jks
ssl.keystore.password=test1234
ssl.key.password=test1234
ssl.truststore.location=/var/private/ssl/kafka.server.truststore.jks
ssl.truststore.password=test1234
```

This way, you can setup SSL authentication for a Kafka cluster.

3.20   How does the linger.ms producer configuration affect Kafka throughput and latency?

The 'linger.ms' configuration for Kafka producers plays an essential role in managing throughput and latency trade-off.

This configuration parameter (which defaults to 0) determines the amount of time (in milliseconds) the Kafka producer will wait in an attempt to batch records together before sending them to the Kafka broker. As a result, the producer sends fewer but more substantial requests, thereby increasing throughput and decreasing the workload of the broker.

In other words, 'linger.ms' increases the latency period in each produce request but at the same time increases the chances for the producer to send messages in batch and reduces the protocol overhead cost for the producer, hence increasing the throughput.

Here is an example of how it can be set:

```
Properties props = new Properties();
props.put("bootstrap.servers", "localhost:9092");
props.put("key.serializer", "org.apache.kafka.common.serialization.
    StringSerializer");
props.put("value.serializer", "org.apache.kafka.common.serialization.
    StringSerializer");
props.put("linger.ms", 5);
Producer<String, String> producer = new KafkaProducer<>(props);
```

However, be cautious with increasing the 'linger.ms' parameter. A higher value might increase the latency, as the producer waits longer and hence messages are not sent immediately upon receipt by the producer. Hence it might not be acceptable in scenarios where low latency is required.

Therefore, deciding on the value of 'linger.ms' for your Kafka producer would need to consider the trade-off between higher throughput (by allowing for more batching) and lower latency.

Chapter 4

Advanced

4.1 How does Kafka's "segmented" log storage work, and what benefits does it offer?

Apache Kafka uses a unique storage mechanism known as "segmented" log storage which is remarkably different from the traditional log storage methods. This system is designed to offer high throughput and efficient data retention for tackling large stream of records prevalent in real-time data processing.

In Kafka, the messages belong to a topic, a stream of records that are divided into partitions. Each partition is an ordered, immutable sequence of records continuously being appended to a structured log. Each record in a partition is assigned a unique offset. Kafka ensures partitioned and fault-tolerant storage of these logs/data across a cluster of servers, making it inherently distributed.

The term 'segmented' refers to the way how Kafka stores these logs. In each partition, the log is split into segments where each segment corresponds to a file in the filesystem. A producer appends new messages towards the end of the last segment file, and each segment file is named after the offset of its first message.

```
TopicA
   Partition 0
      segment 0-0  (offsets 0 through 0)
      segment 1-10 (offsets 1 through 10)
      segment 11-20 (offsets 11 through 20)
      segment 21-30 (offsets 21 through 30)
```

Segmentation offers several powerful benefits:

- **Improved I/O Efficiency:** Since Kafka writes are sequential, having logs broken into segments can drastically improve I/O efficiency. Operating systems always prefetch data when a file is being read, and with segmentation, it reduces the number of unnecessary disk seeks.

- **Efficient data retention:** In Kafka, data retention can be controlled by time, size, and a segmented log makes it much more efficient. The older segment files can be deleted or compacted as per policies, without affecting the newer data.

- **Fault Isolation:** A corruption within a segment file due to bugs or hardware failures can affect only the messages within that segment, preserving the integrity of the rest of the data.

Overall, Kafka's "segmented" log storage scalability, durability and performance characteristics make it ideal for real-time data stream handling.

4.2   Describe the role and functioning of the Kafka Controller.

The Kafka Controller is one of the key parts of Apache Kafka's architecture. It plays a crucial role in the management and coordination of the Kafka cluster. Specifically, the Controller is responsible for:

1. Broker failures: The Kafka Controller takes action whenever there's a broker failure within a Kafka cluster. It ensures the detection of the failure and the triggering of the failover mechanism. This means that it reassigns the leadership of the affected partitions to another replica to maintain the availability of the data stream.

2. Topic partition leadership: The controller decides which broker will be the leader for a topic partition, and it also keeps track of the in-sync replicas for each partition. Whenever a new leader is required (for example, if a broker goes down), the controller will choose a new leader from among the in-sync replicas.

3. Managing and coordinating rebalances: When there is a change in the Kafka cluster such as addition or deletion of brokers, the controller manages the redistribution of topic partitions across the cluster and coordinates the rebalance process.

4. Handling requests like creating, deleting, and scaling topics: The operations like creation, deletion, or modification of topics are handled by the controller. It propagates these changes to the other brokers in the cluster.

To illustrate how a Kafka Controller functions, let's say we have three brokers in a Kafka cluster, and Broker 1 is assigned as the Kafka Controller.

If Broker 1 fails, an election takes place and a new Controller is chosen from the remaining brokers. The new Controller will then handle the responsibility of reassigning the leadership for the partitions where the old Broker was a leader to maintain the availability and reliability of the data stream.

```
// Example code showing how the Kafka Controller might handle a broker failure
public void handleBrokerFailure(int failedBrokerId) {
    Set<TopicPartition> partitionsLedByFailedBroker = getPartitionsLedByBroker
        (failedBrokerId);
    for (TopicPartition partition : partitionsLedByFailedBroker) {
        int newLeaderId = electNewLeaderForPartition(partition);
        if (newLeaderId >= 0) {
            commitNewLeaderForPartition(partition, newLeaderId);
        } else {
            log.error("Failed␣to␣elect␣a␣new␣leader␣for␣partition␣" + partition
                );
```

```
        }
      }
    }
```

(Note: This is a very simplified illustration that doesn't capture all the complexities of the controller's tasks)

The Kafka Controller provides the coordination needed to ensure the resilience and fault-tolerance of the Kafka cluster. It centralizes the metadata management and provides the single source of truth for the state of the Kafka cluster.

4.3   How does Kafka handle unclean leader election, and what are its implications?

Unclean leader election is a feature in Kafka which enables a non-ISR (In-Sync Replica) broker to become the leader of a partition when no previous ISR broker for the partition is available. This can happen during a network partition or a significant broker failure scenario where all the brokers that are part of the ISR for a partition are not available at a given point in time.

While this feature may occasionally help to improve availability, enabling unclean leader election can also have severe implications including the possibility of data loss. This is because a non-ISR broker may not have all the committed messages, hence data may be lost from the point the non-ISR broker takes over as the leader.

Unclean leader election is controlled by the parameter 'unclean.leader.election.enable' in the Kafka configuration. By default, this parameter is set to 'false', meaning that non-ISR brokers are not allowed to become partition leaders.

Below is the pseudocode of how Kafka would behave during an unclean leader election when the above flag is set to 'true':

```
if (ISR.contains(availableReplicas)){
```

```
    leader = ISR.firstOf(availableReplicas);
}else if(`unclean.leader.election.enable` == `true`){
    leader = nonISR.firstOf(availableReplicas);
}
```

As a best practice to prevent data loss, it is generally recommended to keep 'unclean.leader.election.enable' as 'false'. However, in certain situations where availability is preferred over consistency or where data loss can be tolerated, enabling unclean leader election may be an option. It's crucial to carefully assess this trade-off before making a decision.

4.4   Explain the significance of the min.insync.replicas configuration.

The 'min.insync.replicas' configuration is a very significant setting in Apache Kafka's topic-level configurations. It defines the minimum number of replicas that must acknowledge a write for the write to be considered successful when the producer sets 'acks' to 'all' or '-1'. This configuration plays a vast role in controlling the durability of the messages.

Because of how Kafka uses replication for robustness, allowing multiple copies of a message to exist across a cluster, this configuration plays a key role. If a Kafka broker goes down, due to any reason (like hardware failure, network failure, etc.), Kafka still serves the data from the other replicas.

Let's assume the replication factor is set to 3, which means there are three copies of each message of this topic. But suppose that the 'min.insync.replicas' is set to 2. If a producer sends data with 'acks=all' setting and if at only one broker is running, the producer will not be able to write any data, as the 'min.insync.replicas' condition (2 in-sync replicas) cannot be fulfilled.

So, carefully setting min.insync.replicas can help in making sure data durability is maintained and message loss does not occur during the broker failure. However, it is also to note that setting a higher value will affect the availability of writes; as the producer will need to wait for acknowledgments from more replicas, which are possibly on different brokers, the higher value directly affects the overall Kafka cluster's performance.

Here is how you set the configuration:

```
// Set min.insync.replicas through a topic's configuration
AdminClient adminClient = AdminClient.create(props);
NewTopic newTopic = new NewTopic("my-topic", 12, (short) 3) //creating new
    topic
  .configs(Collections.singletonMap("min.insync.replicas", "2"));
adminClient.createTopics(Collections.singleton(newTopic));
adminClient.close();
```

In this example, 'min.insync.replicas' is set to "2" for the topic "my-topic". The topic is having a total of 12 partitions and a replication factor of 3. So, for any write to be successful, at least 2 replicas must send acknowledgments.

4.5   How does Kafka's idempotent producer feature work?

Kafka's idempotent producer feature is designed to ensure that exactly only one copy of each message is written to the broker even when there are retries. It gives stronger semantics in the presence of failures.

Here is how it works:

1. When you enable idempotence ('enable.idempotence=true'), the producer assigns a unique PID (Producer ID) to each new producer instance.

2. It also starts a sequence number, seq, from zero for each topic-partition.

3. For each message that the producer sends, it includes the current PID and seq in the message.

4. The broker maintains the largest sequence number, lastSeq, that it received from each producer for each topic-partition.

5. If the broker receives a message from the producer with a sequence number, seq, that is not exactly one larger than lastSeq, it concludes that a message was lost and it rejects the message.

6. When the producer resends the message, it sends it with the same sequence number as before. So this way, even when a message is resent, it has the same seq and therefore the broker does not count it as a duplicate message.

Here is an example of this setting in a producer's configuration file:

```
props.put("enable.idempotence", "true");
props.put("acks", "all");
props.put("retries", Integer.MAX_VALUE);
props.put("max.in.flight.requests.per.connection", 5);
```

This configuration ensures that even if individual message sends fail and are retried (due to the high 'retries' value), the semantics of the produce call are exactly once. This is due to the fact that idempotence is enabled, and max in flight requests per connection have been reduced from the default to ensure ordering in the face of retries.

Please note that, setting the 'enable.idempotence' to true will automatically set the following configurations:

- 'acks' to 'all'

- 'retries' to Integer.MAX_VALUE

- 'max.in.flight.requests.per.connection' to 5, if the version is less than 2.5. Otherwise, it will set it to 1.

So, we don't need to set them explicitly, if idempotence is required in your producer.

The price you pay is a slight increase in latency and decrease in throughput, but you get higher consistency and reliability in the presence of failures. However, the specified configurations are necessary, as in the absence of these settings this feature could result in out-of-sequence delivery, which is what it's designed to prevent.

4.6   Describe the difference between end-to-end latency and produce/consume latency in Kafka.

In Apache Kafka, both end-to-end latency and produce/consume latency are important metrics that give insight into the performance and efficiency of the Kafka cluster.

1. **Produce/Consume Latency**: This refers to the time taken for a message to be sent (produced) to the Kafka system (from the producer), or the time taken for the consumer to consume (receive) that message. It can be impacted by factors like network latency, Kafka broker performance, serialization/deserialization overhead, etc.

For a producer, it starts when you call the 'send()' method and ends when the broker acknowledges that the record has been appended to the target partition. For a consumer, it begins when a record is sent to a consumer and ends when 'poll()' returns that record.

In short, produce/consume latency measures the time it takes for an individual message to be successfully produced or consumed.

2. **End-to-End Latency**: On the other hand, end-to-end latency in Kafka refers to the time taken from when a message is published to the Kafka topic by the producer, until it is picked up and processed by the consumer. In other words, it includes both the produce and consume latencies, along with the time the message remains in the Kafka system.

End-to-end latency in Kafka directly impacts the real-time processing capabilities of the application. High end-to-end latency can delay the processing of data, causing a ripple effect that can slow down downstream systems.

Thus, end-to-end latency is a broader measure and indicative of the overall system performance, including factors ranging from producer speed, Kafka topic configuration, consumer speed, as well as network speed.

A high end-to-end latency implies either the producer is slow to send messages, the consumer is slow to process them, or the messages are remaining within the Kafka system for too long before being consumed.

Here is a sample code that measures produce latency:

```
long startTime = System.currentTimeMillis();
producer.send(new ProducerRecord<String, String>(topic, key, value));
long elapsedTime = System.currentTimeMillis() - startTime;
```

The same can be done for consume latency. For end-to-end latency, the same method can be applied but over the entire process of producing, the message remaining in the system, and getting consumed.

Note: Measuring these metrics accurately in a distributed and multi-threaded system can be tricky, and it's generally recommended to use Kafka's built-in metrics reporting or an external monitoring system that is designed for such tasks.

4.7   How does Kafka Streams handle stateful operations?

Kafka Streams supports stateful operations such as aggregation, joins, and windowing. To achieve this, Kafka Streams utilizes a local store that maintains the state of streaming data for processing. The local store generates so-called state stores, represented as data structures (like tables or queues) that can be persisted to local or remote storage.

A state store is created either automatically or manually. For example, when performing aggregation operations, Kafka Streams would create a state store automatically. You can also create state stores manually using a StateStoreSupplier.

Let's assume we have a streams operation:

```
KStream<String, String> source = ...; // a KStream
source.groupByKey()
    .windowedBy(TimeWindows.of(Duration.ofMinutes(5)))
    .reduce((v1, v2) -> v1 + v2,
            Materialized.as("reduced-store"));
```

In the above example, when you perform a reduce operation on a windowed KStream, Kafka Streams will automatically create a state store named "reduced-store".

Stateful operations store their resulting data in these state stores. Each task in Kafka Streams gets its own state stores, meaning the operations are isolated and cannot interfere with one another.

To maintain fault-tolerance for these local state stores, the local state is continuously backed up to a Kafka topic behind the scenes. In case of a fault, the state can be restored from the backup Kafka topic. Kafka Streams performs this recovery automatically.

In addition, Kafka Streams provides APIs to query its local state stores, so you can expose the state of your stream processing application via an interactive query.

Here's a rough flow of how Kafka Streams handles stateful operations:

1. The stateful operations compute their data and store it in a state store.

2. The local state of each task in Kafka Streams is continuously backed up to a Kafka topic.

3. In case of failures, the Kafka Streams library recovers the local state from the Kafka topics.

4. The state store API can be queried for the current state of the stream processing application.

This enables Kafka Streams to handle stateful stream processing reliably and in a fault-tolerant manner.

4.8 What are the challenges and solutions for running Kafka in a multi-datacenter setup (mirroring or replication across datacenters)?

Running Apache Kafka in a multi-datacenter setup presents several challenges. Here are some of the prominent ones:

1. **Data Replication:** Kafka relies on the underlying filesystem for data persistence. It does not support explicit data replication across multiple datacenters. High latency links between datacenters can impact replication and partition leadership election, leading to slow performance and increased risk of data loss.

2. **Network Partitions:** Network problems can cause 'split-brain' scenarios where a part of the cluster might believe itself to be the new Kafka cluster and start operating independently, leading to potential loss of data consistency.

3. **Increased Network Costs and Latency:** Running a multi-datacenter setup involves transmitting data over wide area networks (WAN), which is slower and more expensive than local area networks (LAN).

4. **Time synchronization:** Kafka relies on system time for various operations. Any skew in time synchronization can cause problems with broker election, offset retention, etc.

To manage these challenges, several solutions can be implemented:

1. **MirrorMaker or Confluent Replicator for Replication:** Mirror-Maker is Kafka's own tool for cross-cluster data replication. It effec-

tively copies data from source cluster to target cluster. The Confluent Replicator is another tool developed by Confluent, which provides more robust and granular control over data replication.

2. **Stretch Clusters and Virtual Networks:** By creating stretch clusters across datacenters and using virtual networks to improve connectivity, you can reduce network partitions and reduce network latency.

3. **Replica Placement:** Rather than using the default replica assignment strategy, it's more beneficial to carefully design replica placement across datacenters maximizing the data reliability and minimizing replication latency.

4. **Use of Zookeeper:** Zookeeper can manage and coordinate brokers. Since it requires a majority of nodes to be active for operaion, deploying it across datacenters can help in achieving high availability and disaster recovery.

5. **Accurate Time Synchronization:** Use Network Time Protocol (NTP) or other time synchronization services to ensure system clocks on all machines are synchronized.

6. **Increase Replication Factor:** A higher replication factor ensures data availability in case a datacenter goes down.

A well-configured setup will take into account these challenges and will make use of appropriate solutions to handle potential issues. However, managing Kafka in multi-datacenter is no small feat and requires careful planning and continuous monitoring.

4.9   Explain the concept of "sticky partitioning" in Kafka.

The concept of "sticky partitioning" in Apache Kafka is related to a strategy that attempts to minimize the movement of record consumption from one partition to another, effectively reducing network traffic, and sustaining a consistent connection between consumers and Kafka brokers.

When consumers join or leave a consumer group, Kafka needs to re-balance the partition-consumer assignment. This operation could become expensive and negatively impact performance as it will trigger closing/reopening network connections, potential disk I/O operations for retrieving offsets or data, and so forth.

The "sticky partitioning" strategy improves over the previous strategies (Range and Round Robin) by preserving as many existing assignment as possible.

The way it works can be summarized as follows:

1. During a consumer group rebalance, Kafka first identifies which partitions have been currently handled by the consumers that are still alive.

2. It then tries to assign each partition back to its original consumer (as long as that consumer is still part of the group).

3. For any other unassigned partitions (e.g., those belonged to a failed consumer or new topic partitions), Kafka will follow an iterative process that balances the partition assignment across the consumers.

4. During this process, Kafka also ensures that the consumers that had previous assignments will try to get an equal number of the remaining unassigned partitions, hence distributing the load evenly.

This technique leads to fewer partition migrations between consumers during rebalances, and as a result, it provides better performance for Kafka Consumer.

You do not need to explicitly enable "sticky partitioning": it is the default assignment strategy since Kafka version 2.4.

```
// Relevant configuration setting in a Kafka consumer:
props.put(ConsumerConfig.PARTITION_ASSIGNMENT_STRATEGY_CONFIG,
```

```
"org.apache.kafka.clients.consumer.StickyAssignor");
```

Please note that even though this is a better strategy for most cases, there might be scenarios where other strategies (Range or RoundRobin) could become a better fit, such as workflows including only stateless processing or workflows where you would like to prioritize fair partition distribution and can afford frequent rebalances.

4.10 How does Kafka's Exactly Once Semantics (EOS) differ from traditional transactional systems?

Apache Kafka's Exactly Once Semantics (EOS) is a feature that facilitates end-to-end delivery of messages exactly once, guaranteeing that a record will neither be lost nor processed more than one time. This offers a more secure message system compared to at-most-once and at-least-once delivery systems.

To understand how exactly-once semantics differ from traditional transactional systems, it's necessary to divide the operation into two parts: the write phase and the read/process phase.

1. **Write Phase**: Here, Java produces API while providing an idempotent feature which allows you to write the same data multiple times, but it will store only once, thus ensuring the data will precisely produce one time. Transactional write is another crucial aspect where you can write to multiple partitions atomically.

```
// Enable idempotency
props.put(ProducerConfig.ENABLE_IDEMPOTENCE_CONFIG, "true");

// Transactional write
props.put(ProducerConfig.TRANSACTIONAL_ID_CONFIG, "my-transactional-id");
```

2. **Read/Process Phase**: Kafka's EOS differs from other traditional messaging systems by managing 'read' and 'process' of messages in two separate steps. Kafka Streams API guarantees that

messages won't be duplicated using a unique combination of stream tasks (that fetch and process data) and consumer groups (that read data).

```
Properties streamsProps = new Properties();
streamsProps.put(StreamsConfig.PROCESSING_GUARANTEE_CONFIG, StreamsConfig.
    EXACTLY_ONCE);
```

Traditional transactional systems manage the above two aspects at the application level with the help of databases, MQ systems and other resources. However, Apache Kafka integrates all of these into one system. Thus, Exactly Once Semantics in Kafka is not just about sending and receiving messages; it is an end-to-end guarantee between the producer and the ultimate recipient (user/application).

Meanwhile, in traditional transaction systems, two-phase commit protocols (2PC) are employed for achieving exactly once semantics. This method is a distributed algorithm that coordinates all the processes that participate in a distributed atomic transaction on whether to commit or abort the transaction. However, it is known to have shortcomings in terms of availability and performance. Kafka provides strong durability and fault-tolerance guarantees by replicating the data, and decouples the process of reading and processing data, which solves many issues associated with 2PC.

Although Exactly Once Semantics (EOS) increases the overhead in the Kafka cluster because of the validation, deduplication, and retries process, it is well worth it in critical applications where message duplication or data inconsistency cannot be tolerated.

4.11 Describe the role of the transactional.id in Kafka's EOS.

EOs is an abbreviation for exactly-once semantics, a key feature in Apache Kafka that ensures each message is delivered and processed exactly once, thereby preventing any data loss or duplication.

The 'transactional.id' is an essential part of this mechanism. It is a user-configurable string that uniquely identifies a transactional producer. If this ID is the same as a previously-used ID, any ongoing transaction with that ID will be fenced off. This is vital in preventing dual writes caused by producer retries.

A 'transactional.id' has two roles:

1. **For fault recovery:** The 'transactional.id' enables Kafka to recognize when the same producer instance is restarted, such as in the case of an application crash or machine reboot. As it's configured at the producer level, the producer uses the same 'transactional.id' in the event of a restart, and Kafka recognizes this and ensures that any pending transactions from before the restart are completed accordingly.

```
//Initialization of KafkaProducer with Transactional Id
Properties props = new Properties();
props.put("bootstrap.servers", "localhost:9092");
props.put("transactional.id", "my-transactional-id");
KafkaProducer<String, String> producer = new KafkaProducer<>(props);
```

2. **For zombie fencing:** If Kafka detects that a producer with the same 'transactional.id' is writing to a topic, but it has not seen the previous instance of the said producer for the duration specified by 'transaction.timeout.ms', it fences off the older instance to prevent it from writing any further, thus guarding against multiple instances (alive and presumed dead) concurrently writing to the same topic. Zombie fencing is crucial in distributed systems where network issues may lead to "live" producers being presumed dead momentarily but they return to life once the network issue is resolved.

```
//Setting transaction.timeout.ms in KafkaProducer
Properties props = new Properties();
props.put("bootstrap.servers", "localhost:9092");
props.put("transactional.id", "my-transactional-id");
props.put("transaction.timeout.ms", "60000"); // Set producer to timeout after
      60,000ms/1 min
KafkaProducer<String, String> producer = new KafkaProducer<>(props);
```

In conclusion, the 'transactional.id' plays a significant role in facilitating exactly-once processing semantics in Kafka by allowing for transaction recovery and preventing dual writes.

4.12 How do you handle backpressure in Kafka consumers?

Backpressure is a condition where a system is receiving data at a rate higher than it can process. This situation can lead to an overflow of data and can adversely impact the system performance. In Kafka, backpressure can be a challenging situation because Kafka works on a pull-based model and not on a push-based model. Which means, the producer does not have control over the pace at which consumers are consuming the data. Nevertheless, Kafka provides mechanisms to handle backpressure.

The following are the methods to manage backpressure in Kafka:

1. Consumer Configurations: The most immediate way to resolve backpressure is to adjust the consumer's configurations. 'fetch.min.bytes' and 'fetch.max.wait.ms' are two important configurations that can be adjusted.

The 'fetch.min.bytes' parameter sets the minimum amount of data that the broker should return for a fetch request. If the minimum amount of data is not available, the broker waits until the given amount is available before returning the response.

'fetch.max.wait.ms' is the maximum amount of time the broker will wait for the 'fetch.min.bytes' data to become available.

By tuning these configurations, the rate of data fetch by the consumer can be controlled.

2. Increase Consumer Instances: Kafka topic partitions data and multiple consumer instances can read from different partitions simultaneously. Therefore, one way to handle backpressure is to increase the number of consumer instances or the number of threads in each

consumer (if it is a multi-threaded consumer). This increases the
overall processing speed, thereby helping with the backpressure.

3. Adding more hardware resources: If backpressure is a consistent
problem, it might be necessary to scale the systems. More memory,
CPU or disk might be needed for consumers to process faster. If a
single machine does not suffice, then scaling out, i.e., adding more
machines might be necessary.

Here's a basic example of a consumer configuration:

```
Properties props = new Properties();
props.put("bootstrap.servers", "localhost:9092");
props.put("group.id", "consumerGroup1");
props.put("fetch.min.bytes", "10000");
props.put("fetch.max.wait.ms", "20");
props.put("key.deserializer", StringDeserializer.class.getName());
props.put("value.deserializer", StringDeserializer.class.getName());
KafkaConsumer<String, String> consumer = new KafkaConsumer<String, String>(
    props);
```

Theabove example sets 'fetch.min.bytes' to 10000 bytes and 'fetch.max.wait.ms'
to 20 milliseconds. This means the consumer will wait for 20 milliseconds for at least 10000 bytes of data to be available.

4.13 What are the implications of setting the acks configuration to all in Kafka producers?

When we set 'acks=all' in the Kafka producer, it means that the
producer requires a full set of in-sync replica acknowledgments in
response to each record sent. The in-sync replicas are the configured
number of healthy replicas that should maintain the current product
log end offset at any given time.

An 'ack' is a confirmation the producer gets after a write operation.
The producer will consider a message sent only when it receives the
'ack' for that message.

Setting 'acks=all' essentially means that the leader will wait for the full set of in-sync replicas to acknowledge the record. This setting is the most durable, but the slowest setting since it provides the highest data reliability, which becomes handy if you cannot afford to lose any message.

However, this setting has a few implications:

Increased Latency: Since 'acks=all', the producer has to wait for all In-Sync Replica (ISR) to acknowledge receipt. Consequently, the latency in message sends could be higher.

Decreased Throughput: Continued from the above point, as the latency is higher, it leads to lower throughput as the ability to send messages gets slowed down.

Higher Reliability: As all replicas have to acknowledge, the chances of message loss are minimal unless all the Kafka brokers go down at once.

Risk of Blocking: If the number of replications fails to meet the required 'min.insync.replicas' setting, the producer could be blocked.

So, the decision to use 'acks=all' should be made carefully, trading-off between data durability and performance.

Here is an example of how to set it up in your Kafka Producer configuration:

```
Properties props = new Properties();
props.put("bootstrap.servers", "localhost:9092");
props.put("acks", "all");
props.put("key.serializer", "org.apache.kafka.common.serialization.
    StringSerializer");
props.put("value.serializer", "org.apache.kafka.common.serialization.
    StringSerializer");
Producer<String, String> producer = new KafkaProducer<>(props);
```

With the above configuration, the producer will send messages and wait for acknowledgement from all in-sync replicas before sending the next message.

4.14   How does Kafka's KTable differ from KStream in Kafka Streams?

In Apache Kafka's stream processing library, Kafka Streams, there are two abstractions you can use to manipulate data, namely KStream and KTable. The key difference between KStream and KTable is based on Kafka's fundamental model: handling streams of records.

'KStream' is a basic record stream where each data record (also known as message) represents a self-contained datum in the unbounded data set. A KStream object is similar to a regular Kafka topic in that it represents an immutable, unbounded stream of records. We can create new KStream objects from existing KStream objects through operations like map, filter and transform.

Here is how you might declare a 'KStream':

```
KStream<String, String> source = builder.stream("source-topic");
```

Meanwhile, 'KTable' is a table-like structure where each data record represents an update. It can be thought of as a changelog stream, where each data record is interpreted as an insert, upsert or delete action on the table's state. A KTable is a view onto the data in a Kafka topic, where each data record represents an update. The latest update for each key is the current state for that key. You can create new KTable objects from existing KTable objects through transformations such as aggregations and joins.

Here's an example of a 'KTable' declaration:

```
KTable<String, String> table = builder.table("source-topic");
```

So, KStream and KTable serve different needs and will result in different behavior, especially considering time and windowing operations. Note that a KTable could be converted to a KStream and vice versa, by using 'KTable.toStream()' and 'KStream.groupByKey()'.

A 'KTable' can be regarded essentially as a Materialized View, where it maintains the latest value for any record's Key, hence making it possible to handle data as Update/Upserts based on Keys. Whereas a 'KStream' will handle every record as an Immutable data point or Insert.

Hence if there are multiple records in the kafka topic with the same Key, in a KTable representation it will always represent the latest Value for that Key. However in 'KStream' it will treat each of these records as an independent insert even though they might have the same key.

This can be highly useful in scenarios where the same key can have multiple updates and the application is interested only in the current(or latest) State of the Key.

4.15   Describe the process of tuning Kafka for low-latency operations.

Tuning Apache Kafka for low-latency operations is essential in situations where you require real-time data processing. Here are some steps that you can follow to tune Kafka for low-latency operations:

1. **Tune the Time in Kafka Producer:** To minimize latency, it's advisable to set a high throughput and a little time in the Kafka producer configuration. This can be achieved by setting 'linger.ms' and 'batch.size' in the Kafka Producer configuration as:

```
props.put("linger.ms", 1);
props.put("batch.size", 32000);
```

The 'linger.ms' property specifies the time to wait before sending a produce request in case the batch is not full, and 'batch.size' defines the number of bytes of data to collect before sending a produce request. By keeping 'linger.ms' low, we can achieve lower latencies since this would reduce the delay before sending the requests.

2. **Message Compression:** Sending fewer bytes can often help reduce latency. You can choose a compression type on your producer. Kafka supports 'gzip', 'snappy', 'lz4', 'zstd' compression types.

```
props.put("compression.type", "gzip");
```

3. **Replication Factor and In-Sync Replica (ISR):** It is crucial to have the appropriate value of a replication factor for faster recovery from failure, but higher values can contribute to higher latencies. The number of ISRs can also affect latency. If the number of 'min.insync.replicas' is higher, the producer has to wait for a longer time till the message gets acknowledged by all replicas.

4. **Broker Configurations:**

- **num.network.threads:** This is the number of threads that the broker will use to process requests. If your broker is constantly at high CPU utilization, you might need to increase this value.

- **num.io.threads:** This is the number of threads the broker will use for processing file I/O. If your disks are the performance bottleneck, you may need to increase this value.

5. **Acknowledge Mode:** This ('acks') property decides how many acknowledgments the producer requires the leader of Kafka to have received before considering a request complete.

```
props.put("acks", "1");
```

Using 'acks=1' implies that the producer gets an acknowledgment after the leader replica has received the data. This mode can reduce the latency effect.

All these configurations can help tune Apache Kafka for low-latency operations, but remember that these configurations could also affect the other factors in your use case, such as durability, throughput, etc. Make sure to do adequate testing to verify that you have found a good balance for your specific use case. It's also important to monitor your cluster and adjust these configurations as your data volume changes. Each use case will have a different optimal configuration, and the best configuration for you is one that meets your specific requirements.

4.16 How does Kafka handle disk I/O and what optimizations does it employ for efficient storage access?

Apache Kafka employs a variety of strategies to optimize its disk I/O operations and efficiently access storage:

1. **Sequential Disk Access:** Disk access is one of the most expensive operations a system can perform, due to the physical constraints of spinning disks. Kafka optimizes disk I/O by reading and writing to the disk in a sequential manner, which is far more efficient than random access. Kafka stores all its messages in a write-ahead log (WAL), and whenever a message is produced, it gets appended at the end of this log. This results in very high throughput even with cheap, common hard drives.

2. **Zero Copy:** Traditional data transfers usually involve data copying several times within system memory before it gets sent to a network socket or a file system. Kafka avoids this overhead by adopting the "zero-copy" technique, where the operating system copies data directly from the file system cache to the network buffers, eliminating additional copies and system calls. It dramatically reduces CPU usage and increases throughput.

3. **Batching:** Kafka batches multiple small message writes together to form a significant one before writing to the disk. Batching is a common technique used to amortize small disk writes over larger ones for better efficiency. This technique aligns well with the producer and consumer models of Kafka, where several producers can send data to Kafka to batch up and write to disk in one swoop, and similarly, consumers can read data in large batches rather than one message at a time.

```
properties.put("batch.size", 327680);
properties.put("linger.ms", 1);
```

4. **Page Cache:** Kafka relies heavily on the operating system's page cache for its disk I/O operations. It delegates the task of caching to the operating system instead of maintaining a separate cache in the application layer. This leads to reduced garbage collection overhead and better utilization of the available memory. The operating system can directly serve a read request from the page cache if the data resides there, leading to faster responses.

5. **Compression:** Kafka supports GZIP, Snappy, and LZ4 compression codecs which can dramatically reduce the size of the data being written to disk. This leads to more efficient disk usage and faster disk I/O operations. However, it's important to note that while compression reduces the disk I/O, it may increase the CPU usage due to the overhead of compression and decompression.

```
properties.put("compression.type", "snappy");
```

6. **Log Compaction:** Kafka uses a feature called log compaction on topics to mitigate the storage space problem. It retains only the last update for each key within a partition. It ensures that Kafka retains at least the last known value for each message key within the log of data for a single topic partition. It allows a longer retention period for a given dataset size.

```
# Enable log compaction
log.cleanup.policy=compact
```

7. **Indexing:** Kafka maintains indexes for the log files for efficient access. A sparse index file is maintained for every log file consists of a pair (offset, position) indicating each message's position in the log file for a given offset. This allows Kafka to access messages efficiently even in a large dataset.

By using these methods, Kafka can efficiently handle disk I/O and perform read/write operations with high throughput, even on commodity hardware.

4.17 Explain the significance of the max.poll.records and max.poll.interval. ms configurations in Kafka consumers.

'max.poll.records' and 'max.poll.interval.ms' are two important configuration settings for Kafka consumers that provide control over how records are fetched from Kafka brokers.

1. 'max.poll.records'

The 'max.poll.records' configuration controls the maximum number of records that a single call to 'poll()' will return. In other words, it determines the batch size of record consumption from the Kafka topic. The default value is 500.

This can be particularly useful in cases where processing the records can be time-consuming. By limiting the number of records returned, you can ensure that records are not unnecessarily fetched and wasted if they can't be processed in a timely manner. It also helps in managing the memory used by the consumer.

Let's say if your consumer uses intensive computational logic or makes a network call for each message. If you are processing one by one and commit the offset after processing each, setting max.poll.records=1 would make sense.

Here is an example of how to set 'max.poll.records' when creating a KafkaConsumer:

```
Properties props = new Properties();
props.put("bootstrap.servers", "localhost:9092");
props.put("group.id", "test");
props.put("key.deserializer", "org.apache.kafka.common.serialization.
    StringDeserializer");
props.put("value.deserializer", "org.apache.kafka.common.serialization.
    StringDeserializer");
props.put("max.poll.records", "500");
KafkaConsumer<String, String> consumer = new KafkaConsumer<>(props);
```

2. 'max.poll.interval.ms'

The 'max.poll.interval.ms' configuration is used to control the maximum delay between invocations of 'poll()'. It impacts how long a
Kafka broker will wait for the consumer to make a 'poll()' request
before considering the consumer to be dead and beginning to rebalance the consumer group.

If a consumer doesn't call 'poll()' function within this specified interval, then the consumer will be considered as dead and the group
coordinator will trigger a rebalance. The default value is 300000 milliseconds (5 minutes).

This parameter can be used to prevent rebalances if processing can
take longer than the session timeout. Be careful, however, as setting
this value too high can delay detection of failed processes.

Here is an example of how to set 'max.poll.interval.ms' when creating
a KafkaConsumer:

```
Properties props = new Properties();
props.put("bootstrap.servers", "localhost:9092");
props.put("group.id", "test");
props.put("key.deserializer", "org.apache.kafka.common.serialization.
    StringDeserializer");
props.put("value.deserializer", "org.apache.kafka.common.serialization.
    StringDeserializer");
props.put("max.poll.interval.ms", "60000");
KafkaConsumer<String, String> consumer = new KafkaConsumer<>(props);
```

In summary, 'max.poll.records' and 'max.poll.interval.ms' play a critical role in managing how records are fetched and processed by Kafka
consumers, providing knobs to optimize for throughput, latency, and
processing time based on the specifics of your use case.

4.18 How do you ensure data ordering in a Kafka topic with multiple partitions?

In Apache Kafka, topics are divided into partitions for parallelism. Events sent to different partitions can be processed in parallelism. While Kafka guarantees the ordering of messages at the partition level (meaning records sent by a producer to a particular partition will be appended in the order they are sent), there's no built-in global ordering across the multiple partitions of a topic.

For example, if you sent three messages - M1, M2, and M3 in that order, it is guaranteed that M1 will be written to the partition before M2, and M2 before M3. But if these messages get distributed to multiple partitions, there can be scenarios where M2 in partition 1 might be consumed before M1 in partition 0.

To preserve total order across all messages, you can only use a topic with a single partition. But this will limit your throughput to a single machine.

However, assuming you have a workload that can be partitioned, you can ensure Ordering in Multi-Partition Kafka Topic in following ways: 1. Semantic Partitioning - One possible solution is to derive the partition from a semantic feature of the message, which guarantee messages are produced to the same partition in an ordered fashion. For example, if your messages are related to user activities, you can choose to partition by the user ID. This ensures all of a user's activities are ordered. This means load is distributed but ordering is guaranteed within each user.

```
//Producer
ProducerRecord<String, String> record = new ProducerRecord<>("my-topic",userId
    ,"message");
producer.send(record);
```

2. Use a Custom Partitioner - Kafka Producer allows you to specify custom partitioner logic. This logic can be used to direct specific keys

to specific partitions or to implement specific ordering needs.

```
public class CustomPartitioner implements Partitioner {
    @Override
    public int partition(String topic, Object key, byte[] keyBytes, Object
        value, byte[] valueBytes, Cluster cluster) {
        // custom logic to decide partition number
        return partition;
    }
    ...
}
```

Use it while creating a producer,

```
props.put(ProducerConfig.PARTITIONER_CLASS_CONFIG, CustomPartitioner.class.
    getName());
KafkaProducer<String, String> producer = new KafkaProducer<>(props);
```

Please note that this solution can cause uneven load on the Kafka broker as some partitions might have more records than others.

In both cases, Kafka only guarantees order within a partition, not across partitions in a topic. To have total order across all messages, use a topic with a single partition. This will limit your throughput to a single machine.

4.19   Describe the challenges and strategies for managing large-scale Kafka consumer deployments.

Managing large-scale Kafka consumer deployments can pose several challenges. Below are some of them:

1. **Ensuring High Availability and Fault Tolerance:** Kafka instances can fail or network partitions can occur. Ensuring high availability and preventing a single point of failure is vital.

2. **Balancing Load:** For efficiency, it's essential to evenly distribute the consumption of messages across a large number of con-

sumer instances and ensure that each instance is not overloaded or underutilized.

3. **Data Consistency and Ordering:** Ensuring consistent data consumption and maintaining message ordering can be a challenge across multiple consumers due to factors like rebalancing of data partitions among consumers and handling time-sensitive messages.

4. **Scalability:** The Kafka consumer system needs to scale dynamically as the data load varies, adding or removing consumers as needed, without causing performance issues.

5. **Monitoring and Alerting:** In a large-scale deployment, monitoring the health and performance of each Kafka consumer instance, identifying potential issues, and alerting the relevant team can be complex.

To overcome these challenges, you may adopt the strategies below:

1. **Clustering and Replication:** Kafka supports clustering of instances and replication of messages. You can create a Kafka Cluster with multiple brokers and replicate each message to multiple brokers, making data resilient to broker failure.

2. **Partitioning and Consumer Groups:** You can split topics into multiple partitions, ensuring that data is distributed evenly across various Kafka Consumers in a Consumer Group. This way, every message in a partition is sent to exactly one consumer in the group, ensuring load balancing and maintaining the order of consumption.

```
Properties props = new Properties();
props.put("bootstrap.servers", "localhost:9092");
props.put("group.id", "test");
props.put("enable.auto.commit", "true");
props.put("auto.commit.interval.ms", "1000");
props.put("session.timeout.ms", "30000");
props.put("key.deserializer", "org.apache.kafka.common.serialization.
    StringDeserializer");
props.put("value.deserializer", "org.apache.kafka.common.serialization.
    StringDeserializer");
KafkaConsumer<String, String> consumer = new KafkaConsumer<>(props);
```

3. **Auto-scaling:** Based on the workload, you can dynamically

add or remove Kafka Consumers, ensuring your application remains performant and cost-efficient.

4. **Comprehensive Monitoring and Alerting System:** Leveraging tools like Kafka's built-in metrics, JMX, Grafana, and alerting systems like PagerDuty can help keep track of the performance and health of Kafka Consumer instances, identify issues early, and speed up the resolution process.

5. **Custom Partition Assignment Strategies:** Kafka provides flexibility in partitioning including round-robin, range, and custom methods to distribute data across consumers suitable to the specific requirement of the businesses.

These strategies collectively help in building a reliable, efficient, and scalable Kafka Consumer system.

4.20   How do you handle schema migrations in a Kafka ecosystem using tools like Confluent's Schema Registry?

Schema migrations in Kafka ecosystem can be handled by using Confluent's Schema Registry. The Schema Registry is a service that provides a RESTful interface for storing and retrieving Avro schemas.

For a Kafka producer application that sends Avro data, each record has an associated Avro schema. The record's schema is registered with the Schema Registry, which returns a schema id. The Kafka producer can then send the schema id and the Avro-encoded data in a Kafka message. Kafka consumers who respond to the message can extract the schema id from the message, then consult the Schema Registry for the associated Avro schema.

The Schema Registry supports schema evolution, which allows you to update the schema over time. Confluent's Schema Registry pro-

vides backward and forward compatibility checks while registering
schemas, which means you can add new fields to your schema or remove optional fields, and older consumers can still read newer version
of records and new consumers can read older version of records.

Here are the general steps for a schema migration using Confluent's
Schema Registry:

1. Register a new schema with the Schema Registry. If the schema
registration is successful, the Schema Registry will return a new schema
id.

```
SchemaMetadata schemaMetaData = schemaRegistryClient.register(subject,
    newSchema);
```

2. The producer application uses the new schema's id for subsequent
Kafka records.

3. While deploying Schema migration, it is suggested to do a Canary
deployment where you produce messages using the new schema ver-
sion/format in some instances and the older version in others. This
helps in making sure, your system behaves normal and as expected
before doing the complete rollout.

4. The consumer application checks the schema associated with each
Kafka record. If the schema has changed, the consumer retrieves the
new schema using the schema id from the Schema Registry.

```
Schema schema = schemaRegistryClient.getByVersion(subject, version, true);
```

5. Confluent's Schema Registry allows you three compatibility modes
for schema migrations, namely: FORWARD, BACKWARD, and FULL.
You can choose the one that suits your requirements of both producer
and consumer.

You can set them while registering:

```
ConfigUpdateRequest configUpdateRequest = new ConfigUpdateRequest();
configUpdateRequest.setCompatibilityLevel(CompatibilityLevel.FORWARD);
schemaRegistryClient.updateCompatibility(configUpdateRequest, subject);
```

Remember that some constraints, such as nullability, or new required fields, can create compatibility issues. To safely handle schema migrations, it is often recommended to only allow backward-compatible changes, such as field addition or deletion.

By storing schemas in Confluent's Schema Registry, application developers can ensure that their Kafka-enabled applications continue to produce and consume data, even as schemas evolve.

Chapter 5

Expert

5.1 Dive deep into Kafka's storage mechanism. How does it optimize for both writes and reads?

Apache Kafka follows a log-based storage mechanism. This means it stores its messages in a topic as an ordered, immutable sequence of records, also referred to as logs. Each record in a topic has an associated offset, a unique identifier.

Here's a breakdown of how this mechanism optimizes for both writes and reads:

Writes:

1. **Sequential Disk Writes:** Rather than random disk write operations, Kafka performs sequential disk writes. This leads to enhanced throughput and reduces the I/O latencies because it aligns with the nature of hard drives that perform well for contiguous blocks of data.

2. **Zero-Copy Method:** Kafka uses SendFile API for data transfer
directly from the disk socket thereby minimizing CPU copy and context switches. This procedure is known as zero-copy and it enhances
Kafka's performance by reducing the overhead during the write operation.

3. **Batch Writes:** Kafka also writes messages in batches which
reduces the network overhead and enhances throughput. Larger batch
sizes lead to more compression and lesser I/O.

Reads:

1. **Offset-based Lookup:** Kafka retains the offset value for each
message in a log. This allows direct access to specific message loca-
tions, providing efficient reads.

2. **In-memory Indexes:** Kafka maintains two types of indexes in
memory: a time index (for log retention purposes) and an offset index.
The offset index maps offset to file positions, enabling constant time
access to messages during reads.

3. **Zero-Copy Method:** Similar to write operation, for read operation also, Kafka employs the zero-copy optimization to serve data in
the pagecache directly to a network channel, thereby improving read
performance.

Here's a simple representation of Kafka's log structure:

```
+---+---+---+---+---+---+---+---+---+---+---+
| M | M | M | M | M | M | M | M | M | M | M |
+---+---+---+---+---+---+---+---+---+---+---+
  0   1   2   3   4   5   6   7   8   9   10
```

In this log model, each 'M' represents a message, and the numbers
represent the offset. As you can see, each message has a unique,
sequential offset, making it easy to access directly for reads.

By using these methods, Kafka optimizes both writes and reads within
its storage system. This balanced optimization is one of the many rea-

sons why Kafka is preferred as a messaging system for high-throughput, low-latency platforms.

5.2 How does Kafka's "log cleaner" work, especially in the context of log compaction?

Apache Kafka's Log Cleaner is a utility tool that plays an essential role in managing the Kafka log storage. Specifically, in the context of log compaction, the Log Cleaner performs critical tasks in managing and maintaining the space efficiency of Apache Kafka system.

Log compaction in Kafka is designed to solve the problem of data storage. Kafka stores all messages in a log file, and as the number of messages increases, the size of the log file also increases. If not managed properly, these growing log files could overrun the storage available. Hence, log compaction becomes a vital component of Kafka, whose goal is to create a leaner log that holds the latest update (value) for every message key.

- Log cleaning is carried out in the following steps:

1. **Choosing the Log:** The log cleaner first chooses the dirtiest log that has the highest ratio of unnecessary (old and stale) to necessary (latest) messages.

2. **Log Segmentation:** The logs in Kafka are broken down into several segments based on size or time. The log cleaner operates on a per-segment basis. It reads each message from the segment to decide whether to keep it or discard it.

3. **Writing to Destination:** If the record's key is the latest record, it writes the record to a destination log segment file. Other records are discarded. The old segments are replaced by compacted new segments.

4. **Swapping the Active Segment:** The cleaner thread continues to clean other log segments until all the segments in the log (except the active segment) are cleaned.

5. **Throttling:** Log cleaner operations may cause substantial I/O activity and can be throttled according to the configuration to avoid resource saturation.

- Here is an example of the Log Cleaner configuration:

```
"cleanup.policy" : "compact,delete"
"log.cleanup.job.schedule.interval" : 6000,
```

In this configuration, the log cleaner is set up to delete old log segments beyond a certain age, compress them to save space, and compact them to remove older records.

In summary, Kafka Log Cleaner along with log compaction ensures efficient use of storage by removing old and unnecessary messages while only retaining the latest update for each message key,hence making sure that all the consumers of the topic can reconstruct the final state of every keyed message.

5.3   Describe the nuances of Kafka's replication protocol and how it ensures consistency across replicas.

Apache Kafka's replication protocol achieves high availability of data, fault tolerance and consistency across replicas by making use of in-sync replicas (ISR), leaders and followers.

Below are the main nuances of Kafka's replication protocol:

1. **Topic Partitions and Replicas**: Each topic in Apache Kafka is divided into partitions where messages are written. For durability and fault tolerance, Kafka replicates each partition to multiple brokers.

These copies are referred to as replicas. Each partition has multiple replicas, however, there is only one leader replica (responsible for all reads and writes) and the rest are follower replicas.

2. **Leader and Follower Replicas**: For every partition, Kafka selects one broker as the leader, who coordinates the writes and reads for that partition. All other replicas are followers, which passively replicate the leader. When a new message is written, it is stored locally in the leader and then forwarded to follower replicas.

3. **In-Sync Replicas (ISRs)**: A replica is considered in-sync if it's caught up to the leader, i.e., it has copied all messages from the leader that the leader has acknowledged to the producer. ISR is the set of such replicas, which includes the leader. Kafka only considers a message committed when it has been written to all replicas in the ISR. This ensures that committed data is never lost, as long as at least one ISR remains.

Here's a scenario to show how Kafka ensures consistency:

Let's say a producer sends a message to Kafka. First, the leader replica writes the message to its local log. Then, it forwards the message to all follower replicas. When the followers have successfully written the message to their local logs, they send an acknowledgment back to the leader.

The leader waits until it has received acknowledgments from all replicas in the ISR before acknowledging the write to the producer. This means, as long as we have at least one replica in-sync, we won't lose any committed data.

However, what happens if a follower crashes or becomes slow and cannot catch up? If the follower remains behind for long (based on 'replica.lag.time.max.ms' configuration), the leader removes it from the ISR. This follower will not be given any consideration while committing new messages. But it can rejoin the ISR once it catches up with the leader.

This ensures that slow followers do not slow down the leader and overall message commitment. At the same time, we ensure that data is as replicated as possible across the cluster.

And in the event of the leader failing, one of the followers within the ISR will be elected as the new leader, ensuring that data is not lost. This highlights Kafka's efforts in achieving consistency and durability. To ensure such consistency under failing scenarios, it makes use of distributed systems consensus protocol named "ZooKeeper".

5.4   How does Kafka handle network partitions, and what are the potential risks associated with them?

Apache Kafka provides different mechanisms to handle network partitions. Kafka relies on Apache ZooKeeper to underpin the architecture of its distributed system. Zookeeper is a consensus solution that applies an algorithm for fault-tolerant coordination of distributed systems to implement features such as broker leader-election, topic or partition metadata storage and access, etc.

When there is a network partition, usually there is a discrete partition between few of the brokers and the Zookeeper ensemble which results in the brokers in question shutting down the socket connection with the ensemble and hence becoming unresponsive. As brokers disconnect from Zookeeper due to the partition, they lose their Session and Zookeeper triggers an ephemeral node deletion event.

Here is a brief scenario of how Kafka handles network partitions:

- Step 1: ZooKeeper node deletion event notifies Kafka Controller of a broker being down. Due to this, the Kafka Controller initiates a leadership re-election process for the partitions whose leader was present in the lost broker, prior to this event.

- Step 2: The new leaders are elected from the pool of available replicas in the ISR (In-Sync Replica set) list for that partition. Kafka guarantees that committed messages are always present in the ISR set.

- Step 3: Once the network partitioning issue is resolved, and the lost broker comes back, it syncs up with the new leader to obtain all the messages it missed during the partition outage.

Though this mechanism tries to handle partitioning in the best possible way, there are a few risks associated with it:

1. **Data Loss:** If unclean leader election is enabled, data loss might happen due to a follower replica, which might not have all the data, being elected as a new leader.

2. **Increased Latency:** During the network partition, when a broker loses its connectivity with ZooKeeper, it results in message loss and hence retransmission of messages from the producer which causes increased latency.

3. **Split-brain scenario:** In a situation where the brokers are divided into two parts due to network partition, both parts can elect their own leaders, which can lead to inconsistency and data corruption.

4. **Performance:** If there is a network partition, the network can get choked because all the read and write requests will be served by the leaders only, increasing the load on them.

To mitigate these risks, we should always keep in mind to enable minimum.insync.replicas and acks configuration properties. This ensures that at least certain replicas acknowledge to write operation to prevent data loss. Also, it's not recommended to enable the unclean leader election, as it can lead to data loss.

Apache Kafka handles network partition very well, but one must also be aware of the potential risks associated with network partitions to fully exploit Kafka's capabilities.

5.5 Explain the intricacies of Kafka's rebalancing protocol for consumer groups.

The rebalancing protocol used by Kafka consumer groups is important to ensure a fair distribution of topic partitions amongst the consumers (the consumers are also referred to as members) within a consumer group, especially as they join or leave the group, or as the topics' partition count changes.

Here is a detailed breakdown of the protocol:

1. Group Formation: When multiple consumers join a group, all consumers are assigned a unique consumer ID by Kafka. All consumers with the same "group.id" form a consumer group.

2. Rebalance Initiation: A rebalance is initiated whenever there is a change in consumers (a new consumer joins the group, or an existing consumer leaves) or in topic partitions (a new topic is created, a topic is deleted, or a topic's partitions are modified).

3. Partition Ownership: To ensure that a single partition is consumed by exactly one consumer in the group at a time, Kafka assigns a unique owner to every partition. This assignment is done using a strategy function (like round robin or range strategy).

4. Ownership Revocation: When a rebalance occurs, current partition ownerships are revoked and consumers stop fetching data.

5. Partition Reassignment: New partition assignments are done using the strategy function again, ensuring fair distribution and at-most-one consumer per partition policy.

6. Resuming Consumption: Consumers then fetch the saved offset of their assigned partitions from Kafka and resume consumption from the next offset.

7. Handling Imbalances: If a consumer fails to send heartbeat within the 'session.timeout.ms' period, it's assumed dead and a rebalance

will be triggered. 'max.poll.interval.ms' determines how long Kafka waits for a consumer to contact the broker. If no contact is made, Kafka assumes the consumer to be dead, triggering the rebalance.

Kafka rebalancing has a slight impact on processing as during rebalance, consumers are not consuming data. To prevent this from causing noticeable delays in data processing, it's important to plan and configure Kafka's many time parameters ('session.timeout.ms, max.poll.interval.ms, heartbeat.interval.ms') based on your use-case and environment.

Please note that the 'max.poll.interval.ms' and 'session.timeout.ms' are prerequisites for liveness and error detection. Also, 'heartbeat.interval.ms' needs to be set less than 'session.timeout.ms' to ensure that heartbeats are sent before a rebalance is triggered.

The rebalance protocol ensures that in Kafka consumer groups, each partition of data will only be consumed by one consumer and a fair distribution of consumption is maintained, providing fault tolerance and scalability.

5.6 How does Kafka Streams manage state, especially in the context of state stores and changelogs?

In Kafka Streams, every Stream task keeps a local state store that represents the latest state as a concrete table. This state store is mainly used for operations like windowed and tabled joins, aggregates and other tasks that require operation on a state. Kafka Stream's state store is durable and fault-tolerant, meaning that it can recover from failures and continue operating correctly.

The data in the state store is organized into key-value pairs, where the key corresponds to the record key and the value corresponds to the state for that key.

But, the state store is only local to a Kafka Streams task, and exists only in memory and on local disk. If it were to be lost (say in a machine crash), it could not be recovered from the Kafka topic to which the task is consuming records. That's why a changelog topic is used.

The changelog topics in Kafka serve as a distributed and fault-tolerant log for the state stores. Whenever a new record is processed by a stateful operation and it modifies the state store, the state of the key of the new record is sent to the changelog topic. In other words, every change in the state store becomes an entry (a change-log) in the Kafka topic.

By default, Kafka Streams materializes window and join operations into a state store which is backed by a changelog topic. This enables fault-tolerance as the state can be recovered by reading the changelog topic.

Moreover, to minimize latency and to reduce pressure on I/O and network resources, the records are not immediately written to the changelog topic. They are cached and flushed to the topic depending upon buffer memory and commit interval.

For example, if records are processed and result in changes to keys A, A, B, A, C (in that order), upon commit, the changelog topic will contain updates A, B, C for the respective changes.

```
StreamsBuilder builder = new StreamsBuilder();

KTable<String, Long> countedNames = builder
    .<String, String>stream("input-topic")
    .groupBy((key, value) -> value)
    .count(Materialized.<String, Long, KeyValueStore<Bytes, byte[]>>as("
        counts-store"));

countedNames.toStream().to("output-topic", Produced.with(Serdes.String(),
    Serdes.Long())));
```

In the above code example, a state store named "counts-store" is created backed by a changelog topic.

In conclusion, the combination of state stores and changelog topics allow Kafka Streams to manage state in a durable and fault-tolerant manner. Confirm state optimally and automatically by tuning the buffer memory and commit interval based on the use case at hand, whether it emphasizes throughput, latency, storage costs, or fault-tolerance, to name a few.

5.7 Describe the challenges and strategies for operating Kafka at massive scale, e.g., trillions of messages per day.

Operating Apache Kafka at a massive scale, for instance, trillions of messages per day, can present a unique set of challenges. However, there are strategies that one can employ to maintain performance and the overall health of the system.

1. **Challenge: Data Overhead**: The first challenge that comes when working with Kafka at massive scale is the data overhead. This can lead to issues with both storage and network bandwidth.

Strategy:

- Optimizing disk usage: Kafka allows you to compress messages on the fly before they're stored, and most importantly it can serve the compressed messages to consumers. This can significantly reduce the amount of disk usage and can help to store more messages in broker. You can compress your Kafka messages using Gzip, Snappy, or LZ4. Example:

```
Properties properties = new Properties();
// other properties...
properties.put("compression.type", "gzip");
KafkaProducer<String, String> producer = new KafkaProducer<>(properties);
```

- Using a schema management tool like Confluent's Schema Registry to handle message validation and encoding/decoding, which can reduce the size of the message payload and network traffic.

2. **Challenge: Balancing Load**: The more partitions one has, the harder it is to ensure that all brokers in a cluster are equally loaded

Strategy:

- Kafka provides tools to manually alter the number of partitions or replicas for existing topics. By periodically inspecting cluster state and manually reassigning partitions as needed, you can ensure that all brokers are equally loaded.

- Confluent's Auto Data Balancer can automatically monitor and balance the data in your cluster.

3. **Challenge: Proper Partitioning**: Partitioning is a significant aspect of Kafka. The wrong choices can lead to bottlenecks during data processing.

Strategy:

- The simplest practice is to choose a partition key that will randomly distribute data across all partitions, such as a user ID or device ID. However, if you need to maintain the order of certain messages, those messages must be produced to the same partition.

4. **Challenge: Proper Tuning and Configuration**: Improper configuration can easily degrade the performance of a Kafka cluster, especially when operating at massive scale.

Strategy:

- Tune performance of the Kafka brokers using buffer memory, batch sizes, and number of I/O threads.

- Upgrade to the latest Kafka version to leverage new improvements and bug fixes.

- Measure and Monitor: Use Kafka's built-in metrics along with external monitoring tools to understand the behavior of your system and identify bottlenecks.

5. **Challenge: Recovery from Failures**: Failures are inevitable in any large-scale distributed system.

Strategy:

- Always configure replication for your topics. Kafka's in-sync replicas (ISR) feature ensures that committed data is always available in at least one replica.

- Kafka's Unclean Leader Election feature, which is disabled by default from Kafka 0.11.0, prevents data loss by only electing followers as leaders if they have all the committed data.

Achieving high reliability and performance at massive scale is a complex task. It requires both a deep understanding of Kafka's capabilities and a willingness to carefully monitor and tune your deployment.

5.8 How would you handle disaster recovery in a Kafka setup spanning multiple data centers?

Handling disaster recovery in a Kafka setup spanning multiple data centers can be challenging. We must ensure that events that occur in one data center are correctly replicated in others, that we can handle failovers transparently, and that we can recover any lost data if needed.

Here are several critical steps for disaster recovery:

1. **Kafka's built-in Replication:**

Kafka's distributed nature allows it to handle disasters more efficiently. We can handle disaster recovery via Kafka's built-in data replication. We can define multiple replicas for each partition in a Kafka Topic. These replicas live inside different brokers and possibly different racks, and ensure data safety and availability. Even if one broker fails, the data is served by another broker which has the replica of that data.

```
# You can control replication by configuring the replication factor as
    below:
"replication.factor" : "3" # So that 3 copies of data will be available
```

2. **Mirroring in Kafka:**

Another approach is Kafka mirroring. It copies data across multiple datacenters. Mirroring works by setting up a Kafka consumer that consumes messages from the source cluster, and re-publishing those messages to the target cluster.

```
# The Kafka MirrorMaker provided by Apache Kafka can be used to set up
    mirroring:
bin/kafka-mirror-maker.sh --consumer.config sourceClusterConsumer.config --
    num.streams 2 --producer.config targetClusterProducer.config --
    whitelist=".*"
```

3. **Use of Kafka Connect:**

For streaming data between Apache Kafka and other systems Apache Kafka Connect is very effective.

```
connect-distributed.sh connect-distributed.properties
```

4. **Multi-Datacenter Setup:**

We can setup Kafka in a multi-datacenter where we have One "active" datacenter and one "passive" datacenter. The active datacenter is where all reads and writes go under non-failure conditions. The passive datacenter is purely a hot standy: it hosts a fully replicated copy of the data but under normal conditions no data flows in or out.

5. **Backups:**

Regular backups are critical to disaster recovery, as they provide a secondary copy of your data. Backups can be performed at the topic level or at the entire cluster level, using Kafka's administrative APIs.

6. **Monitoring:**

Continuous monitoring and alerting will help us to identify any failures or performance degradation in a timely manner and apply corrective measures. Tools like Prometheus, Grafana, etc. can be used for this purpose.

It is important to test these disaster recovery mechanisms regularly, to ensure they work as expected when needed. In high-sensitive data scenarios, an additional layer of disaster recovery might be needed like using secondary data storage for backup, using database replicas, and so forth.

5.9   Discuss the potential bottlenecks in a Kafka cluster and how you would diagnose and address them.

There are several potential bottlenecks in a Kafka cluster, including:

1. **Network saturation**: Kafka's performance is heavily dependent on the network. If the network bandwidth is saturated, it can limit the throughput of the Kafka cluster. Tools such as netstat, nload, or iftop can be used to monitor network usage.

2. **Disk I/O**: Disk performance can also be a potential bottleneck for Kafka. Kafka persists all data to disk, and a high rate of data consumption can lead to high disk I/O and subsequently degrade Kafka's performance. Tools like iostat can be used to monitor disk I/O.

3. **CPU utilization**: A high CPU usage can also degrade Kafka's performance. This can be monitored using tools like top or htop.

Addressing these bottlenecks often involves a combination of increasing resources (like adding more brokers to the Kafka cluster, or using machines with better network, disk or CPU capabilities) and optimizing Kafka's configuration.

For example, if the network is the bottleneck:

```
- Ensure that `batch.size` and `linger.ms` are correctly configured in the
     producer. Larger batch sizes and/or longer linger times may increase the
     efficiency of network usage.
- Consider enabling snappy or gzip compression when sending messages. This
     can significantly reduce the amount of network traffic, but at the cost
     of additional CPU usage.
```

For disk I/O:

```
- Monitor disk I/O and consider investing in faster disks (like SSDs) if disk
     performance is a problem.
- Consider adjusting `log.flush.interval.messages` and `log.flush.interval.ms
     ` to control the frequency of disk flushes. Be aware that higher values
     can improve disk usage efficiency, but at the risk of longer potential
     data loss windows in the event of a broker failure.
```

For CPU utilization:

```
- If your CPU utilization is high and network 'isnt a problem, consider
     enabling compression at the producer. Message sets are compressed at the
     producer and decompressed at the consumer, which can reduce CPU usage
     on the broker.
- Refer to the Kafka documentation and other resources to ensure your JVM
     settings are properly configured for your specific use case (like `-Xmx`
     and `-Xms` parameters).
```

Remember to carefully monitor the impact of any changes (using the above-mentioned tools plus Kafka's own performance monitoring tools), as the most effective adjustments often depend on the specifics of the use case and environment.

5.10   How does Kafka ensure data locality, and why is it important?

Apache Kafka ensures data locality through a couple of strategies, including data partitioning and replication.

1. **Data Partitioning:** Kafka topics are divided into a number of ordered, immutable partitions. Each partition is saved on a single disk on a broker, which helps to ensure data locality. Partitioning also allows Kafka to distribute and parallelize the consumption of data

across multiple brokers and consumer processes, enhancing system scalability and performance. Here's an abstract example:

```
Topic: Orders
Partition 1: Broker 1
Partition 2: Broker 2
Partition 3: Broker 3
```

2. **Replication:** Kafka replicates each partition across a configurable number of brokers. This replication not only provides fault tolerance and high availability but also ensures data locality. Consumers connect to the broker that has the local copy of the data partition, improving read efficiency. For instance:

```
Topic: Orders
Partition 1: Broker 1 (Leader), Broker 2 (Follower), Broker 3 (Follower)
```

Data locality is important in distributed systems like Kafka for a few reasons:

- **Reduced Network Overhead:** When the data is located on the same node where processing happens, it reduces the need for data transfer over the network, thereby reducing network latency.

- **Increased Throughput:** Data locality can increase the data processing speed, thus improving the system's overall throughput.

- **Fault Tolerance:** Maintaining data across various nodes provides fault tolerance. If one broker goes down, the data can still be accessed from a different broker that holds the replica.

- **System Scalability:** By allowing data to be processed on multiple nodes in parallel, data locality enhances the system's capability to scale with increasing data volume.

These above features make Apache Kafka a scalable, high-throughput, and fault-tolerant system.

5.11 Dive deep into Kafka's quota management system. How does it ensure fair usage across multiple clients?

Apache Kafka uses a quota management system to ensure that resources are distributed fairly among different clients. The quota mechanisms in Kafka allow operators to ensure that a single client or a group of clients does not monopolize broker resources, such as network, CPU, and storage. This helps to prevent resource starvation for other applications and maintains the overall stability of the Kafka cluster.

A quota in Kafka can be defined for client-specific or user-specific communication. A client quota limits resources utilized by all requests from a particular client, identified by its client ID. A user quota, meanwhile, restricts resources used by a principal across all its clients.

At a low level, Kafka's quota management monitors the rate at which clients produce (write records to a topic) and consume (read records from a topic). The two types of quotas are:

1. Network bandwidth quota: The broker configures the rate at which data is sent or received. If a client crosses the configured limit, the broker throttles only the exceeding client without blocking it entirely. This throttling is made by delaying responses to the client-side, allowing the broker side performance to remain unaffected.

2. Request rate quota: This quota limits the CPU usage per client or per user. This is achieved by putting a cap on the number of requests per second from each client or user. If a client exceeds the quota, request handling is delayed.

To define a quota, you can use Kafka's command line interface. Here's an example of defining a quota for a specific client:

```
kafka-configs --zookeeper localhost:2181 --alter --add-config '
    producer_byte_rate=1024,consumer_byte_rate=2048' --entity-type clients
    --entity-name client1
```

This configuration would limit the client 'client1' to produce data at 1KB per second and consume data at 2KB per second.

You can also define a quota for a user like this:

```
kafka-configs --zookeeper localhost:2181 --alter --add-config '
    producer_byte_rate=1024,consumer_byte_rate=2048' --entity-type users --
    entity-name user1
```

It is important to note, the higher quota among client-specific and user-specific configurations gets precedence. For example, if there are two quotas, one for the client id set to 10KB/s and the other for the user set to 100KB/s, the user quota (which is higher) will be used.

5.12 Explain the intricacies of tuning the JVM for Kafka brokers in a high-throughput environment.

Tuning the JVM for Kafka brokers in a high-throughput environment involves adjusting several parameters to ensure optimal resource utilization and avoid outages due to factors such as garbage collection (GC) pauses.

Some of the JVM options that can be configured include:

1. **Heap Size (-Xmx, -Xms)**: Kafka is often bound by the network and the disk, not by the CPU. The default JVM heap size is not optimal. You should set both -Xmx and -Xms to the same value, for example, 50

```
KAFKA_HEAP_OPTS="-Xmx8G -Xms8G"
```

2. **Garbage Collector**: Kafka uses garbage collector to free up memory space. The most commonly used GC is G1GC. Before Java 9, Kafka used CMS (Concurrent Mark Sweep) garbage collector which is good at handling minor GCs. However, due to its lack of ability to

compress old generation space, it may come across a stop the world
scenario in case of major GCs.

```
KAFKA_OPTS="-XX:+UseG1GC"
```

3. **GC Logging Options**: Enable GC logs for an in-depth understanding of the impact of GC on the performance of Kafka brokers.

```
KAFKA_OPTS="$KAFKA_OPTS␣-verbose:gc␣-XX:+PrintGCDetails␣-XX:+
    PrintGCDateStamps␣-Xloggc:<path-to-gc.log>"
```

4. **JVM Performance Options**: Utilize the '-server' flag to ensure
the JVM gets your server's performance configuration.
'-XX:+UseCompressedOops' can improve RAM usage, depending on
the JVM.

```
KAFKA_OPTS="$KAFKA_OPTS␣-server␣-XX:+UseCompressedOops"
```

5. **JMX**: Enable JMX for remote monitoring and managing the
Java Virtual Machine.

```
KAFKA_OPTS="$KAFKA_OPTS␣-Dcom.sun.management.jmxremote␣-Dcom.sun.management.
    jmxremote.authenticate=false␣-Dcom.sun.management.jmxremote.ssl=false␣-
    Djava.rmi.server.hostname=<hostname>"
```

Remember, tuning JVM parameters for Kafka brokers should be
based on the actual situations of your Kafka deployment and hardware specifications. Therefore, adjustments should be made gradually
and the system should be monitored carefully to observe the impact
of the changes.

Also, before using these settings in a production environment, they
should be thoroughly tested under a load that closely matches the
anticipated production load.

To effectively tune the JVM, you should have a deep understanding of GC behavior, Kafka workload characteristics, and the actual
resources available on your machines.

5.13 How would you handle schema evolution in a backward and forward-compatible manner using Avro and the Schema Registry?

Apache Avro supports both backward and forward-compatible schema evolution. Schema evolution refers to the capability to evolve your schemas as business requirements change and adapt, all while maintaining compatibility with older schema versions. This ensures your data continues to be readable and usable even as schemas change overtime.

With Avro, schema evolution is straight forward. A detailed document defining how schema evolution in Avro works can be found at https://avro.apache.org/docs/current/spec.html#Schema+Resolution. However, to make it simpler:

- Backward compatibility: If a schema S can be used to decode data written in a schema S', then S is said to be backward compatible. This means you can add new fields to your schema as long as you provide a default value.

- Forward compatibility: If a schema S is capable of reading data written in schema S', then it is forward compatible. This means you can either remove fields or add fields, and older schemas will still be able to read new data.

The schema registry is a central repository with a RESTful interface for developers to define standard schemas and register them. It provides versioning support and also allows you to check whether your Avro schemas are compatible with your schema registry version.

To handle schema evolution in a backward and forward-compatible manner, we need to:

- Use Avro for schema evolution. Each Avro record has a schema associated with it, defining its structure.

- Maintain consistency by ensuring schemas are registered with the schema registry in your organization.

- Check for compatibility. If you're evolving schema, the new schema must be backward or forward compatible with the older version. The schema registry can check this at the time of registration.

- Version control your schemas. The schema registry versions every registered schema, and provides support for multiple versions to exist concurrently.

Here's a code example of how you can evolve your schema in a backward-compatibility manner.

We start with a simple Avro schema:

```
{
  "type": "record",
  "name": "myRecord",
  "fields": [
    {"name": "name", "type": "string"},
    {"name": "age", "type": "int"}
  ]
}
```

Adding a new field 'address' to this schema in a backward compatible way:

```
{
  "type": "record",
  "name": "myRecord",
  "fields": [
    {"name": "name", "type": "string"},
    {"name": "age", "type": "int"},
    {"name": "address", "type": "string", "default": ""}
  ]
}
```

The field 'address' has been added, and it includes a default value '""'. This ensures that the schema remains backward compatible - older data that don't have the 'address' field can still be read using the new schema.

This is a basic example; in some cases you may need to manage such changes more carefully to ensure compatibility is maintained. That's where the schema registry's compatibility check comes to play. It helps prevent changes being registered that would break compatibility with existing data.

5.14 Discuss the challenges of integrating Kafka with other systems, like databases or stream processors, in a real-time ETL pipeline.

Integrating Kafka with other systems such as databases or stream processors within a real-time Extract, Transform and Load (ETL) pipeline indeed has some challenges:

1. **Data Consistency**: Consistency across systems is a major challenge. For instance, if you have to sync Kafka with a database in real-time, you have to ascertain that both systems reflect the same data at any given point.

Kafka provides a Connect API for streaming data to and from Kafka either from/to an existing system. Usually this is used for database syncing. For data courtesy, Kafka Connect source connectors include a timestamp with each Kafka record indicating when the data was stored in the source system. But it's not always easy to make both systems consistent especially when there are failures or delays, which happens quite often in distributed systems.

2. **Data Transformation**: Another challenge lies in data transformation. Kafka data is serialized; therefore, it needs to be deserialized before processing. Also, the data formats used by source systems and target systems may vary. Transforming data from one format to another in real-time can be challenging.

Kafka Streams can be used to do the transformations and processing before the data is sent to other systems. But this needs additional coding and testing efforts, and adds complexity.

3. **Latency**: System and Network latencies can affect real-time data processing. The delay in consuming messages from Kafka, processing and storing in some other system can real-time processing challenging.

Kafka has a "producers send data to brokers" and "consumers pull data from brokers" model. This means that when Kafka fetches data, the fetch request data size and time are configurable. If these values are not well-tuned, it can increase latency.

4. **Scalability and Elasticity**: Scaling the ETL pipelines can be challenging especially when data volume grows. It's very hard to scale relational databases while Kafka is designed to be scalable using Kafka's stream processing.

5. **Failures and Error handling**: Handling errors and failures is another great challenge. If some system fails or an error occurred during processing, ensuring data does not get lost or duplicated can be tough.

Kafka provides at-least-once delivery semantics but it introduces the possibility of duplicate messages. So, your application should be designed to handle such scenario.

6. **Resource and Capacity planning**: The resource and capacity planning for such system can become complex based on the system workloads. If the resources (CPU, memory, disk etc) are not planned properly, it could result in performance issues.

7. **Security**: Integration of Kafka with other systems may require sharing of security credentials and other sensitive information among various systems. This could expose potential security risks.

Kafka provides security features like SSL for encryption, SASL for authentication but security setup could be challenging.

5.15 How does Kafka's rack-awareness feature work, and why is it important for large-scale deployments?

Kafka's rack-awareness feature allows you to assign brokers to specific racks in your data center. This helps to make Kafka resistant to entire rack failures, which is incredibly important for large-scale deployments as it ensures that the loss of a single rack doesn't impact data availability.

At the heart of this feature is the concept of replica placement. When a Kafka topic is created with replication factor 'n', Kafka makes 'n' copies of each partition of that topic. Without rack-awareness, Kafka places these replicas on any available broker, with no consideration of their physical location.

However, in a large-scale deployment where you might have dozens or even hundreds of brokers spread across multiple racks, this approach can lead to scenarios where all replicas of a specific partition reside on the same rack. If this rack goes down, that partition becomes unavailable, causing a disruption in service.

This is where rack-awareness comes in. If properly configured, Kafka can intelligently place replicas across multiple racks, ensuring that even if a whole rack goes down, at least one copy of each partition is available on a different rack.

The configuration itself is straightforward. Each broker has a 'broker.rack' setting in its 'server.properties' file. This setting should be given a unique value for each rack, e.g. 'rack1', 'rack2', etc. Then, when creating a topic, you specify a '–replica-placement' policy. This is a JSON file that tells Kafka what your rack setup looks like and how it should place replicas.

Here's an example replica placement policy:

```
{
  "version": 1,
```

```
"replicaAssignments": [
  {
    "topic": "my_topic",
    "partition": 0,
    "replicas": [1, 2, 3],
    "logDirs": ["any", "any", "any"],
    "rack": "rack1"
  },
  {
    "topic": "my_topic",
    "partition": 1,
    "replicas": [4, 5, 6],
    "logDirs": ["any", "any", "any"],
    "rack": "rack2"
  }
 ]
}
```

This policy tells Kafka to place the first set of replicas ('1, 2, 3') for partition 0 of "my_topic" in "rack1", and the second set of replicas ('4, 5, 6') for partition 1 in "rack2". Consequently, even if "rack1" goes down, partition 1 would remain available because it has replicas in "rack2".

In conclusion, Kafka's rack-awareness feature is crucial for large-scale deployments as it ensures high data availability and fault tolerance. It achieves this by spreading data replicas across multiple racks, thereby reducing the risk of data loss or service disruption in the event of a rack failure.

5.16   Describe the potential security vulnerabilities in a Kafka setup and how you would mitigate them.

Apache Kafka is a powerful distributed streaming platform, but like any complex system, it does have potential security vulnerabilities. These vulnerabilities can be mitigated by employing best security practices and configuring Kafka correctly. Here are some potential security issues you could encounter in a Kafka setup and ways to mitigate them:

1. **Data Leakage**: Without proper access controls, unauthorized clients might get access to sensitive data. This could be mitigated via implementing authentication (SASL or SSL) and authorization (ACLs).

1.1 **Authentication**

SASL/PLAIN could be used if all the brokers are trusted. But, to avoid sending credentials in clear text over network, SASL/SCRAM should be used as it is more secure than PLAIN.

Alternatively, for mutual authentication, SSL could be implemented.

```
# Enable SSL
listeners=SSL://:9093

# Location of key store
ssl.keystore.location=/var/private/ssl/kafka.server.keystore.jks

# Password for key store
ssl.keystore.password=test1234

# Password for key
ssl.key.password=test1234

ssl.client.auth=required
```

1.2 **Authorization**

Kafka's Access Control Lists (ACLs) should be used to restrict who can produce or consume from each topic.

```
# Granting producer and consumer access to user "John"
bin/kafka-acls --authorizer-properties zookeeper.connect=localhost:2181 --
    add --allow-principal User:John --producer --topic Test-Topic
bin/kafka-acls --authorizer-properties zookeeper.connect=localhost:2181 --
    add --allow-principal User:John --consumer --topic Test-Topic --group
    test-group
```

2. **Unrestricted Access**: By default, Kafka brokers are accessible from any client. Arbitrarily, any system on the network can send messages, consume data, or even delete data. To mitigate, we can set up firewall rules to restrict which servers or IP addresses can access the Kafka brokers.

3. **Data Tampering**: Without proper security, data could be

tampered while on transit. To prevent this, Kafka supports SSL for encrypting the data if required.

4. **Denial of Service**: Kafka isn't immune to DoS attacks where a malicious client could produce more data than the broker can handle. Configuring quotas on the producers could help to prevent this issue.

5. **Untrusted Code Execution**: If consumers or producers run arbitrary untrusted code, they could affect the Kafka brokers. Validate all inputs to consumers and producers can help to prevent this issue.

6. **Zookeeper Exposure**: Zookeeper, if not correctly managed, could be exploited to disrupt the whole Kafka cluster. Therefore, limiting ZooKeeper's exposure only to necessary Kafka nodes can avoid this potential risk.

Security in Apache Kafka is a vast topic, with many settings and configurations that can be optimized to prevent security threats. Regular upgrades, keeping up-to-date with Apache Kafka's CVEs, and constant vigilance can be very helpful in maintaining a secure Kafka stream. However, it's important to carefully analyze security needs and apply principles of least privilege to thwart potential intrusion attempts.

5.17 How would you design a Kafka-based system to ensure GDPR compliance, especially the "right to be forgotten"?

Designing a GDPR compliant system using Apache Kafka requires planning and a structured approach. In terms of the "Right to be Forgotten" aspect of GDPR, it demands that users have the right to request the deletion of their personal data.

Here is how you can handle this using Apache Kafka:

1. **Data Separation**: It's recommended to separate user-identifiable information (PII) from the rest of the data in a Kafka message. This means Kafka should not store PII directly. Instead, use a unique identifier (a non-identifying UUID for example) to tag messages in Kafka and store the PII in a separate secure datastore. When the "right to be forgotten" is invoked, you only need to delete the PII from the secure data store.

```
Kafka Message = {
  "user_id": "unique_UUID_v4",
  "event": "..."
}
```

In Backend datastore:

```
User Data = {
  "id": "unique_UUID_v4",
  "first_name": "John",
  "last_name": "Doe",
  "email": "johndoe@example.com",
  ...
}
```

2. **Compaction**: Kafka allows for a method of retention known as compaction which only retains the last message produced for a specific key (user identifier in this case), all previous messages can be removed.

3. **Consumer Updates**: All consumers of the Kafka topic should be equipped to handle "delete" events. These events are indicated by a null-valued message in Kafka. When a delete is detected, the consumer should expunge the user data it has stored in its system.

4. **Data Encryption**: To further enhance security, the data in Kafka can be encrypted both at rest and in transit. This can be done using Kafka's inbuilt support for SSL/TLS and disk encryption.

5. **Audit Logs**: Keep track of all data processing and deletion requests in an immutable audit log. This helps to provide evidence of compliance.

It's important to note that collaboration between all systems and processes is key to achieving GDPR compliance. Every system involved in the data processing pipeline must respect the "right to be forgotten" and must be capable of safely deleting user data when required.

Bear in mind that while I've given an overview, GDPR compliance can be complex depending on each individual use case, and you may need to take additional steps to fully comply with all regulations and laws. Always consult with your legal team when dealing with PII and GDPR regulations.

5.18   Discuss the trade-offs between using a compacted topic versus a non-compacted topic.

Apache Kafka maintains the state of all messages or records using a feature known as Topic Log Compaction. This feature allows Kafka to store a dense snapshot of the most recent values for each key in a record instead of the entire log of all messages.

Here are the trade-offs you should consider for using compacted topics vs. non-compacted topics:

1. **Data retention**:

Non-compacted topics operate on a time or space-based data retention logic. Messages will be discarded after a specific time period, or when the storage size hits specified threshold, regardless of the message importance. The fact that the data is impermanent can be a disadvantage in certain situations.

On the other hand, compacted topics keep at least the most recent value for each key. Old records with a key get replaced by new records with the same key. This can be beneficial to retain the latest snapshot/state of data.

2. **Storage space**:

Non-compacted topics can consume more storage space relatively as they store all messages up to retention time. The storage continues to grow as long as new messages are coming into the topic.

In contrast, compacted topics can significantly reduce the storage space as they only store the latest value for each key. So, it inherently provides a mechanism to limit disk usage per topic.

3. **Performance**:

With non-compacted topics, the performance of reading can degrade over time as the volume of data grows.

In compacted topics, the performance of reading the latest value for each key can be optimized since the number of redundant records is minimized. But, log compaction also introduces overhead of scanning and compacting logs, which can possibly affect Kafka's performance.

4. **Data Recovery**:

For non-compacted topics, data once passed the retention period is lost permanently.

Compacted topics can be useful for recovery in many scenarios as they maintain a full snapshot of final record states.

Example for creating a Compacted Topic: "'bash ./kafka-topics.sh –create –bootstrap-server localhost:9092 –topic my-compacted-topic –partitions 1 –replication-factor 1 –config "cleanup.policy=compact" "' Here, "cleanup.policy=compact" specifies that the topic should be compacted.

Overall, the choice between compacted and non-compacted topics heavily depends on the use case and specific application requirements. An appropriate decision can lead to optimized resources utilization and application performance.

5.19 How would you monitor and ensure the health of a Kafka cluster, especially in terms of latency, throughput, and availability?

There are several ways to monitor and ensure the health of a Kafka cluster. Here are some of the possible techniques:

1. **Latency**: You can compute the end-to-end latency as follows:

```
End-to-End Latency = Produce_Time -(Fetch_Response_Max +
    Log_End_Offset_Lag_Max)
```

You can fetch these metrics using either Kafka's built-in metrics via JMX or via external tools such as LinkedIn's Burrow that monitors latency in Kafka.

2. **Throughput**: You can monitor throughput using native Kafka metrics including "MessagesInPerSec", "BytesInPerSec", and "BytesOutPerSec". You will be able to see how many messages are being produced, how many bytes are being sent, and how many bytes are being consumed per second.

3. **Availability**: You can ensure Kafka's availability by detecting and recovering from faults automatically. This involves constantly monitoring for failures and reconfiguring the system whenever a component fails. To monitor broker availability, you can look at the "UnderReplicatedPartitions" metric. If this is greater than zero, then it indicates that at least one broker is down.

For an effective monitoring strategy, consider integrating Kafka with monitoring tools such as Prometheus and Grafana. Prometheus can scrape metrics from your Kafka cluster, while Grafana can visualize this data in user-friendly dashboards.

There are also broker-level metrics that can be useful for Kafka health monitoring:

- 'kafka.network.RequestMetrics': Tracks request-related statistics such as the request rate, request size, response rate, response size, etc.

- 'kafka.network.RequestChannel': Provides statistics about request queues.

- 'kafka.server.ReplicaManager': Helps to analyze replica statistics including UnderReplicatedPartitions, ISRShrinksPerSec, and ISRExpandsPerSec. These are specifically used to evaluate data replication and consistency.

Monitoring tools like Prometheus can be configured to periodically fetch these metrics and Grafana can be set up to display them in a comprehensive dashboard for an overall understanding of Kafka's health and performance.

In addition, it's also important to set up alerts based on these metrics to identify and solve potential issues proactively. Tools like AlertManager in conjunction with Prometheus and Grafana can be used to set up such alerts via Email, Slack, etc. based on the severity and quickness of response required.

5.20   Dive deep into Kafka's time-indexed storage. How does it enable efficient message retrieval based on timestamps?

Apache Kafka primarily relies on two low-level storage mechanisms: offset index and timestamp index, making it unique in how it manages and retrieves records (messages). Understanding these mechanisms can help clarify how Kafka retains massive amounts of data for prolonged periods efficiently, and how it can fetch it quickly.

The Offset index file keeps a mapping between message offsets and their respective position in the log file. Kafka uses this index file to jump to the approximate position in the log file where messages start, and then scans the records until it finds the exact position of the desired message.

The Timestamp index, on the other hand, maps the message timestamps to their respective offsets. This index mechanism makes Kafka efficient in retrieving messages based on timestamps.

When a ProduceRequest arrives, the server would append records to the end of the current log file while also appending entries to the index files (both offset and timestamp indexes). It's important to understand that the entries in the index files are sparse, meaning Kafka doesn't index every message but rather periodically creates an index entry for every n messages to avoid using too much memory.

Now, consider a scenario where you want to find and fetch all the messages after a particular timestamp in Kafka. Here is the sequence of steps Kafka follows:

1. Kafka first uses the Timestamp index to find a mapping between the target timestamp and the closest smaller equal offset.

2. After obtaining the mapped offset, Kafka then uses the Offset index to find the exact position in the log file corresponding to that offset.

3. Kafka then jumps to that position in the log file and sequentially scans through the rest of the records, comparing the timestamps with the target timestamp.

4. The scan will stop when Kafka finds the first message with a timestamp larger than the target timestamp, consequently returning all the messages from this point onwards.

This mechanism provides a highly efficient way of fetching messages based on timestamps.

To illustrate the above in code level, in Apache Kafka (source code), the 'TimeIndex' class in 'LogSegment.scala' represents a time-index file in the log. The 'lookup' method in this class is used to lookup an offset by target timestamp.

```
def lookup(targetTimestamp: Long): TimestampOffset = {
  maybeMeat(targetTimestamp).getOrElse {
    // If no entry found in index, fall back to file end offset with unknown
        timestamp
    TimestampOffset(RecordBatch.NO_TIMESTAMP, baseOffset + sizeInBytes)
  }
}
```

This script attempts to find an entry. If it doesn't find any, it falls back to the file end offset with an unknown timestamp. The 'lookup' method is used by the 'findOffsetByTimestamp' method in 'LogSegment.scala', which provides an interface to find an offset by target timestamp in Kafka segments.

Chapter 6

Guru

6.1 Describe the internal workings of Kafka's segment and index files in its log storage mechanism.

Apache Kafka uses a distributed storage system for its messages. A topic, which is a particular stream of data, is divided into partitions. Each partition is a sequence of records that is continually appended to a structured commit log. The records are each assigned a sequential ID called an offset.

In the Kafka ecosystem, partitions are split into smaller units called segments. A segment is nothing more than a set of messages, and it corresponds to a logical offset vector inside a partition. Each segment corresponds to two physical files in the OS:

1. Log file (.log): This file stores actual messages. 2. Index file (.index): This file stores an index to locate messages within the log file.

These are both allocated in advance to a size specified by the 'log.segment.bytes' configuration.

In order to serve up records efficiently, Kafka compresses the records into a batch format and stores them in a file called a segment. A segment is a simple, append-only log file, and each segment file is associated with an index file, which maps offsets to record positions.

The index file is a sparse file: not every message has an entry, only those messages at the start of each 'n' position, where 'n' is a configurable number of bytes. The consequence of this is that in order to find a message, the process may need to scan from the last index entry up to the position of the desired offset. This sounds inefficient, but because Kafka maintains messages in batches, it typically amounts to very little I/O.

The index file is stored in an OS page cache, which enables very fast access. When Kafka has to search for a message, it first finds the segment with the highest offset that is less than the target offset. Then it scans the index file to find the offset that is nearest but less than the target offset. Finally, Kafka scans the log file from the position in the previous step until it finds the exact offset.

This combination of segment and index files allows more efficient data retrieval and also enables older segment files to be deleted when they expire based on time or size retention policies, which helps limit the storage use.

6.2   How does Kafka's producer batching mechanism work under the hood, and how does it affect latency and throughput?

Kafka's producer can send records to the broker in batches, a feature that contributes significantly to its ability to handle high volume throughput. Instead of sending records one at a time, which can be time-consuming and expensive in terms of network bandwidth, the producer collects a batch of records and sends them together.

Under the hood, there are two primary settings that determine how the producer batches records:

1. 'batch.size': This is the maximum number of bytes that a batch can accumulate before it's ready to be sent. When this threshold is reached, the batch is sent regardless of how much time has passed since the first record was added. This is good for throughput because network requests are expensive and it's more efficient to send fewer larger batches. However, this means there can be some extra latency since records can wait in the batch until it's full.

2. 'linger.ms': This is a delay that tells the producer to wait up to that many milliseconds for more records to arrive in order to fill up the batch before sending it. Setting a linger delay can increase latency because it introduces an artificial delay, but it also increases throughput because it allows more time for records to arrive and fill up the batch.

For example:

```
Properties props = new Properties();
props.put("bootstrap.servers", "localhost:9092");
props.put("acks", "all");
props.put("delivery.timeout.ms", 30000);
props.put("batch.size", 16384);
props.put("linger.ms", 1);
props.put("buffer.memory", 33554432);
props.put("key.serializer", "org.apache.kafka.common.serialization.
    StringSerializer");
props.put("value.serializer", "org.apache.kafka.common.serialization.
    StringSerializer");

Producer<String, String> producer = new KafkaProducer<>(props);
for(int i = 0; i < 100; i++)
    producer.send(new ProducerRecord<String, String>("my-topic", Integer.
        toString(i), Integer.toString(i)));

producer.close();
```

In this example, the producer will wait until either it has 16384 bytes to send ('"batch.size"') or 1 millisecond has passed ('"linger.ms"'), whichever comes first.

These two settings provide a way to trade-off latency and throughput. If you want to prioritize latency, you can lower 'linger.ms' (or set it to 0) and lower 'batch.size'. If you want to prioritize throughput, you can increase 'linger.ms' and 'batch.size'.

The producer also has an in-flight requests buffer where it keeps all requests that have been sent but not acknowledged yet. The size of this buffer is controlled by 'max.in.flight.requests.per.connection' property, and it allows Kafka to maintain high throughput even in environments with high latency.

6.3 Discuss the intricacies of Kafka's ISR shrinking and expansion. How does it maintain data integrity during these operations?

In Apache Kafka, ISR stands for In-Sync Replica. Kafka maintains a list of ISRs for each topic partition. The producer waits for acknowledgments from all in-sync replicas or ISRs, indicating that they have received the data. This ensures data durability and high availability in case of failure scenarios.

The ISR list includes all the replicas that are fully caught up with the leader (which is also a replica). ISR shrinking or expansion refers to Kafka's procedure of removing (shrinking) or adding (expansion) replicas to/from the ISR list.

ISR Shrink:

ISR shrink happens when a replica lags behind the leader. The replica lags could be due to a network partition, slower disk, higher CPU usage, or any other issues causing delays. When a replica hasn't fetched data for a specified amount of time ('replica.lag.time.max.ms'), it gets removed from the ISR list. This helps prevent indefinitely waiting for slow replicas and guarantees data is available as soon as possible on majority of replicas.

```
if (time.milliseconds() - replica.lastCaughtUpTimeMs > replicaLagTimeMaxMs)
    outOfSyncReplicas += replica
```

ISR Expansion:

ISR expansion happens when a previous lagging replica catches up to the leader. If a follower replica is in sync with the leader, it gets added back to the ISR list. This ensures that the in-sync replicas are always ready to take over if the leader fails.

```
if (replica.logEndOffsetOffset >= smallestLogEndOffset && !inSyncReplicas.
    contains(replica))
    inSyncReplicas += replica
```

Data Integrity during ISR Shrinking and Expansion:

Kafka ensures data integrity during ISR shrinking and expansion in the following ways:

1. **Durability**: Data durability is maintained as Kafka waits for acknowledgments from all in-sync replicas to ensure they all have the same data. So, if a replica is removed from ISR, the producer waits for acknowledgment from the new ISR list. The producer will not get an acknowledgment until the data is written to the new ISR list.

2. **Fault-tolerance**: When a faulty replica is removed from ISR, it prevents that faulty replica from being elected as leader during a leader election. This way, the faulty replica will not serve stale or incorrect data.

3. **Read-after-write consistency**: Kafka guarantees that once a write has been acknowledged, it should be readable from all the in-sync replicas.

4. **Availability**: ISR shrink and expansion helps in maintaining high availability of the system. By removing slow replicas from ISR, it

ensures that writes are not blocked. And by adding caught up replicas back to ISR, it ensures that there are enough healthy replicas to take over in case of a leader's failure.

6.4 How does Kafka's delayed fetch operation work, and how does it optimize for large-scale message consumption?

Kafka's "delayed fetch" operation is a cornerstone of the efficient, large-scale message consumption that Kafka is known for. This optimized design is driven by the consumer pull model adopted in Kafka, in which consumers pull messages from brokers when they are ready to process them, rather than brokers pushing messages to consumers. The "delayed fetch" operation is particularly handy to deal with small fetch requests and optimize the overall performance of the Kafka system.

Suppose a consumer sends a fetch request to a Kafka broker, but the data that meets the requirements of the fetch request is not in the broker at this time, indicating that the size of the data is less than the minimum number of bytes requested by the consumer ('fetch.min.bytes').

In this case, the broker uses a "delayed fetch" operation: it does not immediately return the currently available data to the consumer. Instead, the broker holds the fetch request until enough data is available or a certain amount of time ('fetch.max.wait.ms') has passed.

By doing these delayed fetches, Kafka enhances efficiency and reduces resource consumption in a couple of key ways:

- Kafka can reduce the network I/O caused by insufficient data fetch and increase the throughput of Kafka.

- By aggregating multiple small fetches into a big one, Kafka can utilize the disk sequential read capability, which significantly improves the disk

I/O performance.

Code example for fetch request setting in the properties of the Kafka consumer:

```
Properties props = new Properties();
props.put("bootstrap.servers", "localhost:9092");
props.put("group.id", "test");
props.put("enable.auto.commit", "true");
props.put("auto.commit.interval.ms", "1000");
props.put("session.timeout.ms", "30000");
props.put("fetch.min.bytes", "50000"); // minimum bytes the broker must have
    before it responds to fetch request
props.put("fetch.max.wait.ms", "300"); // maximum delay the broker will wait
    before responding to fetch request
props.put("key.deserializer", "org.apache.kafka.common.serialization.
    StringDeserializer");
props.put("value.deserializer", "org.apache.kafka.common.serialization.
    StringDeserializer");
KafkaConsumer<String, String> consumer = new KafkaConsumer<>(props);
```

In this example, 'fetch.min.bytes' is set to 50000 and 'fetch.max.wait.ms' is set to 300. This would inform Kafka Broker to wait until there are 50000 bytes of data to send. If 50000 bytes is not achieved within 300 milliseconds, it will send whatever it has and not wait any further.

6.5   Dive deep into Kafka's request/response protocol. How does it ensure efficient communication between clients and brokers?

Kafka's request/response protocol is a key part of its efficient communication system between clients and brokers. This protocol utilizes an application-level request-reply pattern, with the client submitting a request to a Kafka broker and then waiting for the broker's response.

Here's how it works:

1. **Request**: All requests in Kafka are sent from a client to a broker using a special format that contains the following elements:

- Request type: Identifier of the API (Produce, Fetch, Metadata, Offset, etc.).

- Request version: To handle changes in the protocol.

- Correlation id: Unique integer id that matches the request with the response.

- Client id: Allows brokers to track the source of the request.

- Request-specific fields: Particular fields dependent on the type of request.

For instance, in a Produce request, the additional fields could be topics to send data, records for each topic, etc. Here's an example of a Produce request (pseudocode):

```
ProduceRequest request = new ProduceRequest.Builder(
  string "clientId", // client id
  integer 1, // correlation id
  array<ProduceRequest.TopicEntry> [
  // array of topics
  new ProduceRequest.TopicEntry("topicName1", array<ProduceRequest.
      MessageSetEntry> [
    // array of message sets
    new ProduceRequest.MessageSetEntry(0, array<byte>[...]) ])
  ]).build();
```

2. **Response**: Each request results in a response from the broker, which also has a standardized format:

- Correlation id: Matching the id of the request that generated this response.

- Response-specific fields: These are unique to the type of request that was made.

In a Produce response, specific fields may include the topics that were written, their partitions, and any potential errors. Here's an example of a Produce response (pseudocode):

```
ProduceResponse response = new ProduceResponse(array<ProduceResponse.
    TopicEntry>[
  // array of topic entries
  new ProduceResponse.TopicEntry("topicName1", array<ProduceResponse.
      PartitionEntry>[
    // array of partition entries
    new ProduceResponse.PartitionEntry(0, Errors.NONE.code()) ])
```

```
]);
```

This request/response protocol is highly efficient because:

- **Asynchronous**: Kafka's protocol is asynchronous, meaning that a client can send multiple requests to a broker without needing to wait for a response after each one, thereby enhancing throughput.

- **Batching**: Kafka's protocol supports batching, so multiple records can be included in a single request or response. This helps reduce the overhead associated with sending many small packets.

- **Titanic buffers**: Kafka's protocol uses large, fixed-size buffers that align well with OS-level page caches, making it excellent at handling large data payloads.

- **Forward compatibility**: The versioning feature in request/response protocol ensures forward compatibility. Newer clients can communicate with old brokers and vice versa.

This combination allows Kafka to handle high-volume, real-time, reliable message transmission and streaming.

6.6 Discuss the challenges and strategies of running Kafka in a hybrid cloud environment.

Apache Kafka is an open-source, distributed event-streaming platform capable of handling trillions of events a day. It provides real-time data feed, fault-tolerant storage, and leaps forward in processing speed. Running Kafka in a hybrid cloud environment adds to its complexity. Here are some challenges and possible strategies for dealing with them:

1. **Data Security and Compliance:** The hybrid cloud environment results in data scattering across different clouds and on-premise servers. Ensuring optimum security and adherence to data regula-

tions can be challenging.

Strategy: Leverage Apache Kafka's data encryption, SSL/TLS and SASL features for securing data in transit. Advanced data management features in Confluent's Apache Kafka distribution, such as Role-based Access Control (RBAC), can also be utilized.

2. **Data Integrity and Durability:** Retaining the durability and integrity of data while migrating between on-premise and cloud can be challenging.

Strategy: The Kafka Connect's MirrorMaker can be utilized for replicating, migrating, and ensuring data durability and integrity.

3. **Service Availability and Consistency:** To ensure data is consistently available across the hybrid cloud environment, network outages, latency, and distributed systems' complexities must be managed very well.

Strategy: By utilizing a multi-region Kafka cluster and employing methods like stretch clusters, one can ensure high availability and prevent data loss.

4. **Networking and Connectivity:** Communication between on-premise Kafka brokers and applications running in the cloud can be a challenge due to varied and disjointed networks.

Strategy: Utilizing Direct Connect or VPN solutions to establish a secure and consistent networking environment can be beneficial.

5. **Resource Provisioning and Scalability:** In a hybrid cloud setup, managing resources optimally and scaling according to the demand is important, but often it can be difficult.

Strategy: You can manually add or remove Kafka brokers to deal with scalability issues. However, integration with Kubernetes with the help of Strimzi operator for Kafka accelerates scaling, recovery and provides seamless integration with the hybrid cloud environment.

6. **Operations Management:** Managing complex multi-environment setups generally takes a lot of effort and time.

Strategy: Using self-managed solutions like Confluent for Kubernetes provides operational efficiencies, helping to automate rollouts, rollbacks, and common operational tasks.

It is worth noting that picking the right Kafka distribution that catifies the hybrid cloud environment is crucial. For example, Confluent Kafka offers a completely packaged solution that provides support for a hybrid cloud environment, making it easier to handle certain challenges associated with it.

6.7   How does Kafka's under-replicated partitions metric work, and what are its implications for data integrity?

Kafka's Under Replicated Partitions metric is an essential artifact to keep an eye on in a Kafka cluster. This metric gives the count of partitions where the in-sync replica count is less than the total replica count. In other words, it keeps track of the number of partitions that have not been fully replicated to all the brokers that should have a copy of that partition data in an ideal scenario.

Replication is an essential mechanism in Kafka to prevent data loss. If a broker fails and it is the only one holding the data for one of your topics, that data is lost forever. To tackle this, Kafka uses a replication factor. However, replication in Kafka is not always instantaneous. There might be a lag in data catching up to all the replicas. These replicas that are not in complete sync with the leader are called out-of-sync replicas, and their corresponding partitions are referred to as under-replicated partitions.

The Under Replicated Partitions (URP) metric indicates the number of such partitions which are not fully synchronized across all replicas.

If this metric's value is greater than zero, it implies that there is a risk of data loss if the proper brokers go down. Moreover, Kafka will not allow producers or consumers to read or write to topics with under replicated partitions to ensure strong data integrity.

For checking this metric we can use the Kafka broker level metric 'UnderReplicatedPartitionCount' as follows :

```
kafka.server:type=ReplicaManager,name=UnderReplicatedPartitions
```

Since data is a crucial part of any service or application using Kafka, having under-replicated partitions would be an unacceptable risk. It is ideal to act quickly if this value increases to reduce potential data loss and maintain highest data integrity. Efforts should be placed in tuning the cluster appropriately to ensure a healthy state and low replication lag, which will keep the under-replicated partitions as low as possible.

6.8 Describe the internal workings of Kafka's rate limiter when quotas are enforced.

Apache Kafka's quota feature allows operators to define the amount of data a client (producer or consumer) can send to or receive from a broker within a given timeframe. If the client exceeds the specified quota, Kafka will delay the response to throttle the client's request rate.

The implementation of this feature primarily centers around the Quota class and the ClientQuotaManager. Each client is assigned a sensor to measure the request rate (byte-rate). The checkQuota method is called each time a request is made from the client to monitor the rate at which the client sends/receives data.

In Kafka, rate is calculated as the number of bytes sent or received per second, and the rate computation window is defined as the time period over which the rate is calculated. This window is implemented as a sliding time window that moves every second.

The interesting part is how Kafka handles situations where a client exceeds its quota. When the client's request rate surpasses the quota, the client's sensor will trigger a quota violation. After this, Kafka uses the throttleTime method to compute the amount of time it should delay the response, which is the excess byte-rate divided by the quota.

Overall, Kafka's approach to rate limiting follows a delayed response model to avoid server resource starvation because of one or multiple abusive clients. Kafka doesn't refuse requests from clients violating quota, but serves them with delayed responses.

Here's a simplified example of the underlying logic governing Kafka's client quota enforcement:

```
if sensor.checkQuota():
    throttleTime = sensor.quotaViolation() / quota
    response.delay(throttleTime)
```

Kafka's rate limiter and quota enforcement system provide a valuable mechanism for managing resource utilization in the broker, thereby promoting system stability and performance under various load scenarios.

6.9   How does Kafka Streams handle late-arriving data in the context of windowed operations?

In Kafka Streams, windowed operations such as aggregations and joins are performed based on the timestamps of records. If a record arrives late and falls outside the window it was supposed to be part of, it will not be included in the calculations for that window.

Handling late-arriving data is a critical factor for many stream processing applications. Kafka Streams handles this issue through its window retention period, which is a configurable setting allowing a window to still accept records for some time after the window end time. This period is controlled by the parameter 'retention.ms', and defaults to 24 hours.

If a record arrives after the end of a window but within the retention period, Kafka Streams will include this data in the operation and update the results accordingly. However, if the record arrives after the retention period, it's considered too late and will be discarded.

Example of setting the window retention in Kafka Streams:

```
TimeWindows.of(Duration.ofMinutes(5)) // Creates a window of 5 minutes
        .grace(Duration.ofMinutes(1)) // Sets a grace period of 1 minute
        where late-arriving records will still be processed
        .until(Duration.ofMinutes(10).toMillis()) // Sets the retention
        period to 10 minutes. Any record arriving more than 10 minutes
        late will be discarded
```

In the above example, a window has a duration of 5 minutes and retains records for up to 10 minutes. Additionally, a grace period of 1 minute is set for new records after a window has closed. If a new record arrives within this 1-minute grace period, Kafka Streams will include the record in the window's results and will update the results for that window. However, if a new record arrives more than 10 minutes after the window, it will be discarded.

It's important to note that in Kafka 2.1.0 and later, the grace period defines how long to wait for out-of-order records for a window, as well after the window, before suppressing the results. This can improve the accuracy of the window operation results by reducing the effect of late-arriving data.

Remember that longer window retention and grace periods will consume more storage in your Kafka Streams application as it needs to keep the records longer in memory or on disk. Thus, it is important to balance between system resources and the accuracy of windowed operations in your particular use case.

6.10   Discuss the intricacies of setting up and tuning Kafka's in-built monitoring tools like Kafka Exporter and JMX.

Apache Kafka provides several in-built monitoring tools which can help you gain visibility into Kafka's core performance, operational health metrics and other insights about your Kafka clusters. Two such significant tools provided by Kafka are Kafka Exporter and Java Management Extensions (JMX).

1. Kafka Exporter:

Kafka Exporter is an open-source tool that fetches information from a Kafka cluster and exports it to a Prometheus monitoring tool. It provides many valuable Kafka cluster metrics like consumer group offset, broker status, topic size, and other statistics.

To set up Kafka Exporter:

- First, download and install Kafka Exporter from the GitHub repository.

- Configure Kafka Exporter by specifying your Kafka cluster's address and other configurations in a YAML or JSON file.

- Finally, start Kafka Exporter. It will start fetching metrics from your Kafka cluster and export it to Prometheus.

Here is an example of how to run Kafka Exporter:

```
./kafka_exporter --kafka.server=kafka:9092
```

In this command, '–kafka.server' flag is used to specify the address of your Kafka cluster.

2. JMX:

JMX (Java Management Extensions) is a technology that allows you to implement management interfaces for Java applications. JMX in Kafka can be used to expose Kafka's performance metrics, tune

Kafka's performance, and debug issues.

To use JMX with Kafka:

- Ensure that JMX is enabled in your Kafka broker configuration. You can do this by setting 'JMX_PORT' environment variable to the JMX port you want to use. For example, 'export JMX_PORT=9999'.

- Some Kafka JMX attributes are not registered by default. You can enable them by setting 'KAFKA_JMX_OPTS' in your Kafka configuration. For example, you can set '-Dcom.sun.management.jmxremote.authenticate=false -Dcom.sun.management.jmxremote.ssl=false'.

You can also use JConsole (a GUI tool that comes with JDK) to connect to Kafka's JMX server and browse the JMX metrics.

To tune Kafka's performance using JMX, you can configure several performance-related attributes like heap size, garbage collection settings, and others. For example, you can set the maximum heap size by using '-Xmx' option in 'KAFKA_JMX_OPTS'.

Remember, setting up and tuning these tools are critical tasks and require proper understanding of Kafka's internals and these tools. Always test your configurations in a test environment before applying them in production.

6.11   How would you design a Kafka system to handle multi-tenancy at a massive scale?

Designing a Kafka system to handle multi-tenancy at a massive scale involves an understanding of several factors such as partitioning, replication, low latency, and scalability.

Here is a possible multiple steps design approach:

1. **Partitioning:** Kafka topics are divided into partitions. This

allows for the processing power of a topic to be distributed across multiple nodes. For handling multi-tenancy on a massive scale, effective partitioning schemes are needed. Messages sent to different partitions can be processed in parallel, providing high throughput and scalability.

```
TopicPartition topicPartition = new TopicPartition("topic",
    partition_number);
consumer.assign(Arrays.asList(topicPartition));
```

2. **Replication:** To ensure high availability and fault tolerance, Kafka uses replication effectively. Each partition can be replicated across multiple brokers, thus, even if one broker goes down, another broker can serve the data.

```
bin/kafka-topics.sh --create --zookeeper localhost:2181 --replication-
    factor 3 --partitions 1 --topic topic
```

3. **Isolation of resources:** Differentiate resources for different tenants. This includes isolated CPU and memory resources on the Kubernetes pod, Disk isolation can be achieved by setting up quotas per tenant, Network Isolation can be achieved through network policies for different namespaces representing different tenants, and Kafka's native quota management can be used at the tenant level.

4. **Consumer Groups:** Kafka supports the concept of consumer groups to allow a pool of consumers to divide up the work of processing records. When multiple consumers are subscribed to a topic and belong to the same consumer group, each consumer in the group will receive records from a different subset of the partitions in the topic.

5. **Fine-grained access control:** Kafka provides ACLs (Access Control Lists) to control who can produce or consume from a topic, or who can use certain consumer groups. With ACL, we can ensure that different tenants only have access to their own relevant data.

6. **Monitor and tune Kafka brokers:** Ensure Kafka brokers are properly configured for handling huge throughput and many connections. Monitor the performance indicators such as Under Replicated Partitions, Request handler idle ratio, Network processor idle ratio,

JVM heap usage and garbage collection, etc.

7. **Schema Management:** Considering the massive scale, there could be a scenario where different consumers would require different types of messages. Hence Schema Registry and Avro can be used together, this will allow adding multiple schemas to a Kafka Topic.

8. **Load Balancing:** When some brokers are more occupied than others, the cluster is not balanced and thus leads to inefficient use of resources. Be sure to maintain proper load balancing. Kafka's tool (Kafka-reassign-partitions) can be used for this.

In conclusion, designing a Kafka system for multi-tenancy at a large scale requires a deep understanding of Kafka's internal architecture, its features, and also the capability to effectively tune several parameters to meet the needs of multiple tenants. This is just a high-level approach and would need adjustment based on the specific needs of your workloads and environments.

6.12   Dive deep into Kafka's controller failover mechanism. How does it ensure cluster stability during such events?

The Apache Kafka Controller is responsible for managing the lifecycle of topic partitions. It is one of the Kafka brokers and handles leader election for partitions when there is a broker failure, it also manages and track the replication of input data, and reassign replicas when needed to ensure high availability and durability.

Each Kafka cluster has a unique controller. When the controller goes down, another broker is automatically elected as the new controller. This process is known as controller failover.

Here's how controller failover mechanism works:

1. **Zookeeper Watches**: In Apache Kafka, all brokers are in continuous communication with Zookeeper, which is the centralized service for maintaining configuration information and providing distributed synchronization. The election process of a new controller is influenced by Zookeeper Watches. Each broker has a Zookeeper watch on "/controller" znode. On controller creation or deletion, all the brokers receive a notification.

2. **Broker death & Re-election**: When the current controller detects that it has lost its connection with Zookeeper, it resigns (if it hasn't died). At the same time, all brokers get notified of a change in the controller znode, and they all try to become the new controller by creating a new ephemeral node "/controller". The one which succeeds in creating the node becomes the new controller.

3. **Replica Reassignment**: When a new controller is chosen, it runs the 'onControllerResignation' command on the old controller and starts the replica reassignment process and leader election for all the partitions.

4. **Shutting down the Broker**: If the old controller is still alive when the new controller starts operations, it will finish any operation it is currently running, and stop any new operations from starting, ensuring a smooth transfer of responsibilities.

By successfully implementing the controller failover mechanism, Kafka ensures amongst other things: guaranteed message delivery, no message duplication, and seamless failover which all lead to increased stability and reliability of the Kafka cluster during such events. The whole process of controller failover and replica reassignment is supposed to be transparent to the clients and other brokers with minimal impact on performance or throughput.

6.13   Discuss the challenges and solutions of integrating Kafka with legacy systems in a real-time data migration scenario.

Apache Kafka is an open-source platform for managing real-time data feeds with a publish-subscribe model. Kafka is often used for real-time data migration, ETL (Extract, Transform, Load), and real-time analysis. This high-throughput platform is well-suited for handling huge amounts of data in real-time.

However, integrating Kafka with legacy systems in a real-time data migration scenario can pose several challenges:

1. **Legacy System Drift**: Older systems may not be 'event-driven' or compatible with Kafka's real-time message-based model. Often, legacy systems operate based on periodic scheduling like daily or hourly batches, which is different from Kafka's continuous streaming model.

2. **Data Transformation**: Legacy systems might be using out-of-date or non-standard data formats. Translating these formats to Kafka-compatible formats may be challenging.

3. **Performance Impact**: Legacy systems may not be designed to handle the high rate of data flow that Kafka streams support. This could impact the overall performance of the legacy system.

4. **Capacity Planning**: Kafka requires planning in terms of message size, throughput, retention, and topics' number. Incorrect estimations can affect system performance and resource utilization.

To counter these challenges, here are few approaches:

1. **Using Kafka Connect**: Kafka Connect is a tool for scalably and reliably streaming data between Apache Kafka and other data systems. It makes it simple to quickly define connectors that move

large collections of data into and out of Kafka.

2. **Data Transformation Middleware**: If a direct connection between the legacy system and Kafka is not feasible or efficient, we can use middleware ETL tools to extract data from the legacy system, transform it into a Kafka-compatible format, and then load it into Kafka.

3. **Use a Debezium**: Debezium is a Kafka connector that can stream changes from databases (MySQL, PostgreSQL, MongoDB, etc.) into Kafka, which is suitable for capturing changes in legacy databases.

4. **Throttling**: By applying back pressure and throttling techniques, we can prevent high data rates from overwhelming our legacy system.

5. **Capacity Planning**: Following Kafka's best practices while configuring Producer, Broker, and Consumer configs like batch.size, linger.ms, buffer.memory, fetch.max.bytes, max.partition.fetch.bytes, etc. would help in optimal utilization of resources.

Remember, the best approach largely depends on the specifics of your legacy system and its compatibility with Kafka.

For example, a solution might be as follows:

```
from kafka import KafkaProducer
producer = KafkaProducer(bootstrap_servers='localhost:9092')
producer.send('test', b'Hello, World!')
producer.send('test', key=b'message-two', value=b'This is Kafka-Python')
producer.flush()
producer.close()
```

The above Python code sends data to a Kafka topic named 'test'. You might place this code into a middleware application that transforms and forwards data from your legacy system to Kafka.

6.14   How does Kafka's end-to-end encryption work, especially in the context of inter-broker communication?

Kafka supports end-to-end encryption with the help of SSL/TLS for communication between clients (both producers and consumers) and servers (topic leader and follower brokers). You can use encryption in transit and at rest to ensure data security.

Here is a high-level overview of how Kafka encryption works:

1. **SSL (Secure Sockets Layer) / TLS (Transport Layer Security):** Kafka uses SSL/TLS to encrypt data. The data being sent is encrypted by the sender and can only be decrypted by the recipient using a shared key. With SSL/TLS, data is safe during transfer between client to broker or between brokers. When considering inter-broker communication, every broker should have both the keystore and truststore to encrypt and decrypt the messages for secure communication.

2. **KeyStore:** In the context of Kafka, a KeyStore is required to store private keys, and it is used during the SSL handshake process for encryption. Here, the encryption happens with the help of the recipient's public key.

3. **TrustStore:** A TrustStore is used to store certificates to prove that the network connection can be trusted, meaning the Kafka broker validates against the public keys in the truststore during the SSL handshake process.

To enforce SSL for inter-broker communication, Kafka provides a property named 'ssl.security.protocol' in the 'server.properties' file.

To enable SSL, you can add the below properties in the 'server.properties' file:

```
ssl.keystore.location = /var/private/ssl/kafka.server.keystore.jks
ssl.keystore.password = test1234
```

```
ssl.key.password = test1234
security.inter.broker.protocol = SSL
ssl.truststore.location = /var/private/ssl/kafka.server.truststore.jks
ssl.truststore.password = test1234
ssl.client.auth = required
```

In this example, the 'security.inter.broker.protocol' is set to SSL, meaning that all inter-broker communication will happen over SSL.

Furthermore, to avoid man-in-the-middle attacks, Kafka can also use SSL for client authentication with the broker. If 'ssl.client.auth' is set to required, it forces the client to present a valid SSL certificate in order to connect to the broker.

Finally, SSL can also be leveraged in the context of Kafka Connect and Kafka Streams applications. Similar configurations should be applied to these components as well.

6.15   Describe the potential challenges and strategies for running Kafka on Kubernetes at scale.

Running Apache Kafka on Kubernetes at scale presents several challenges due to the intricacies of both systems. Here are some potential hurdles and the strategies to overcome them.

1. **StatefulSet scalability**: Kubernetes StatefulSets are used to manage Kafka Brokers. Scaling up StatefulSet isn't much of a problem as Kubernetes will sequentially deploy new Pods. However, scaling down is not straightforward since deleting a Pod could cause re-assigning of partitions which affects the performance heavily.

- **Solution**: Design the appropriate partition strategy carefully and providing adequate storage space can result in lower partition reassignments when you are scaling down.

2. **Persistent volumes**: By using StatefulSets for Kafka Brokers,

each Pod gets linked with a Persistent Volume Claim (PVC). If a broker goes down accidentally, Kubernetes recreates the Pod but the volume might take longer to get ready than the Pod, which would cause Kafka broker failure again.

- **Solution**: Using a Kubernetes feature that waits for the PVC before starting the Pod can be considered to account for this problem.

3. **Zookeeper dependency**: Kafka uses Zookeeper for managing and coordinating brokers. Zookeeper can become a single point of failure and managing it separately can get complex.

- **Solution**: Using an operator like Strimzi can help to manage Zookeeper. Strimzi Operator is an open-source project that uses the operator pattern to manage Kafka clusters on Kubernetes.

4. **Network performance**: Kafka extensively uses the network to replicate data between brokers. Any network latency may degrade the Kafka performance. Kubernetes overlay network adds additional latency and overhead.

- **Solution**: Choose networking solutions that are performant and use network policies for securing the Kafka cluster. Some users choose to turn off the overlay network and use the physical network directly.

Here's an example of deploying Apache Kafka on Kubernetes using Strimzi.

```
apiVersion: kafka.strimzi.io/v1beta1
kind: Kafka
metadata:
  name: my-cluster
spec:
  kafka:
    replicas: 3
    listeners:
      plain: {}
      tls: {}
    config:
      delete.topic.enable: "true"
      log.retention.hours: "168"
      offsets.topic.replication.factor: "3"
      transaction.state.log.replication.factor: "3"
      transaction.state.log.min.isr: "2"
    storage:
      type: jbod
      volumes:
```

```
    - id: 0
      type: persistent-claim
      size: 100Gi
      deleteClaim: false
  zookeeper:
   replicas: 3
   storage:
     type: persistent-claim
     size: 100Gi
     deleteClaim: false
  entityOperator:
   topicOperator: {}
   userOperator: {}
```

However, individual circumstances and requirements might require different solutions and different ways of deploying Apache Kafka on Kubernetes.

6.16   How would you handle global state management in Kafka Streams, especially in a multi-region deployment?

Global state in Kafka Streams consists of a globally replicated, read-only Kafka topic and its state stores. This allows Kafka Streams applications to build and leverage tables that are distributed and replicated across all instances.

The global state management is done by defining a 'GlobalKTable' in Kafka Streams applications. The mechanism uses GlobalKTables to keep the full data locally in every instance of the app, hence the name "global".

Defining a GlobalKTable might look as follows:

```
StreamsBuilder streamsBuilder = new StreamsBuilder();
streamsBuilder.globalTable("global-topic", Consumed.with(Serdes.String(),
    new CustomSerde()));
```

The 'GlobalKTable' is backed by an internal 'RocksDB' instance for fast storage and access.

When it comes to a multi-region deployment, the management of global state becomes tricky because Kafka Streams applications might have to fetch data from global tables located in different regions.

In order to efficiently manage the global state in Kafka Streams applications across multiple regions, you can leverage Kafka's MirrorMaker tool. MirrorMaker can be used to replicate topics between the Kafka clusters in different regions. This means you can maintain a copy of the global table in every region and Kafka Streams applications can access them with the same consumer latency as accessing local tables.

However, for multi-region deployments, careful configuration needs to be done with regards to replication factors, and the 'acks' and 'min.insync.replicas' settings, to ensure fault tolerance and data durability.

It's also crucial to monitor the synchronization and replication between the different regions. This is required to ensure that the replicated global state data is up-to-date and available for Kafka Streams applications.

Here is a summary of steps to handle global state management in multi-region deployment:

1. Define a 'GlobalKTable' in your Kafka Streams application.

2. Use Kafka's MirrorMaker tool to replicate global topics between different regions.

3. Configure Kafka's replication factors and data durability settings carefully to ensure consistent state.

4. Regularly monitor the synchronization and replication between the different regions.

Also, it should be noted that using MirrorMaker comes at a cost of increased data transfer between data centers, which could incur additional bandwidth costs. Take this into consideration when designing the architecture.

Remember that handling global state in Kafka Streams, particularly in a multi-region deployment, is a topic worth studying in depth. Many subtle issues can impact the correctness and performance of your streaming applications.

6.17 Discuss the intricacies of setting up and managing a Kafka MirrorMaker deployment for cross-cluster replication.

Setting up and managing a Kafka MirrorMaker deployment for cross-cluster replication involves a thorough understanding of Apache Kafka, MirrorMaker, and related components.

Apache Kafka MirrorMaker is a utility for replicating data between two Kafka clusters. It's typically used in situations where you want to maintain a backup of a Kafka cluster or to migrate data from one cluster to another.

To set this up, there are a lot of intricate steps to be followed:

1. **Two Kafka Clusters:** Firstly, Kafka MirrorMaker requires two active Kafka clusters. One acts as a source cluster from where the data will be replicated and the other one acts as the target cluster where the data will be replicated to.

2. **Configure Consumer on Source Cluster:** In the source Kafka cluster, MirrorMaker needs to consume the data. So, we need to set up a Kafka consumer in MirrorMaker pointing to the source cluster. This can be done using the Kafka consumer properties file.

```
bootstrap.servers=source-cluster:9092
group.id=mirror_maker_consumer
```

3. **Configure Producer on Target Cluster:** Simultaneously, we will have to set up a Kafka producer which will produce the data to

the target cluster. This is done through a Kafka producer properties
file.

```
bootstrap.servers=target-cluster:9092
```

4. **Set up MirrorMaker:** Now, with both Kafka consumer at
source cluster and a producer at target configured, we need to setup
MirrorMaker.

```
bin/kafka-mirror-maker --consumer.config sourceClusterConsumerConfig.
    properties --producer.config targetClusterProducerConfig.properties --
    whitelist=".*"
```

The above command will run MirrorMaker, which will start consuming data at source and producing at the target.

To manage a Kafka MirrorMaker:

- **Monitoring:** It needs regular monitoring to ensure that the data
replication is happening as expected. We should monitor both source
and target clusters actively.

- **Failover and Recovery:** In the event of failure, MirrorMaker
should be able to failover and recover from where it left.

- **Handling Large Volume:** Depending on the volume of data, we
might need to increase the number of MirrorMaker instances. This
is because a single instance might not be able to maintain a high
throughput with large volumes of data.

- **Security:** In terms of security, we will have to ensure that MirrorMaker has the required authorizations on both source and target
clusters.

Remember, with Kafka 2.4.0 onwards LinkedIn has introduced MirrorMaker 2.0 which has been designed to address limitations of MirrorMaker 1. It has several advantages like topic configuration synchronization, automatic topic creation, and preserving of messages
order during failovers etc. Hence, it's advisable to use MirrorMaker
2.0 for cross-cluster replication.

6.18 How does Kafka's priority-based request handling work, especially in the context of ensuring low-latency for critical operations?

Kafka's priority-based request handling is designed to ensure low-latency for critical operations, even under practices of heavy load. This is achieved using two key strategies: priority-based request queuing and quota-based throttling.

1. Priority-Based Request Queuing: Kafka brokers maintain two request queues: a regular queue for normal traffic and a priority queue. When a message arrives, the broker first checks if it belongs to a user or a client that has low-leverage or low-priority. For these regular users, the requests are processed in a round-robin fashion from the regular queue.

Sensitive users or high-priority users' requests are put in the priority queue and are given preference for processing, which ensures low latency. This is particularly important when you have a set of consumers or producers whose operation is more critical than other users.

Here's some pseudo-code for Kafka request handling:

```
class KafkaBroker:
    def __init__(self):
        self.standard_queue = Queue()
        self.priority_queue = Queue()

    def receive_message(self, message, user):
        if user.is_high_priority():
            self.priority_queue.push(message)
        else:
            self.standard_queue.push(message)

    def process_message(self):
        if not self.priority_queue.is_empty():
            return self.priority_queue.pop()
        return self.standard_queue.pop()
```

2. Quota Based Throttling: Kafka also enforces quotas to limit the broker resources used by clients. A client can have producer byte-

rate quota and consumer byte-rate quota. This is done to prevent a high-traffic client from monopolizing the broker's network resources.

Quotas in Kafka is typically defined in bytes/second. For example, if a producer client's quota is set to 10MB/sec, Kafka will try to throttle the network bandwidth used by the client to around 10MB/sec.

Kafka controls the pace of clients by keeping track of a "byte-rate" which is calculated as the average over some window of time. If a client exceeds its byte-rate limit, Kafka will delay the response to cause the client to slow down, effectively achieving throttling.

By combining priority request queuing and quota-based throttling, Kafka ensures low latency for critical operations while smoothly handling large amounts of traffic.

6.19   Describe the challenges and solutions of ensuring GDPR and CCPA compliance in a Kafka-based data platform.

Maintaining General Data Protection Regulation (GDPR) and California Consumer Privacy Act (CCPA) compliance in a Kafka-based data platform presents multiple challenges:

1. **Data Mapping**: Individual's data can be spread throughout different topics and partitions in Kafka. Identifying and mapping these is a challenge. 2. **Right of Access**: GDPR and CCPA require companies to provide individuals with access to their data. With Kafka's distributed, partitioned nature, retrieving all data for a single individual may be difficult. 3. **Right to be Forgotten**: Erasing an individual's data in response to a GDPR or CCPA request is tricky with Kafka, given its immutable log data structure. 4. **Data Minimization**: Storing only necessary data is a key principle of both GDPR and CCPA. Making sure data streams don't

contain excess personal data can be challenging. 5. **Consent Management**: Managing, tracking, and enforcing consent related decisions with regard to data processing in real-time can be complex with a Kafka-based data platform. 6. **Data Security**: Ensuring secure data processing and communication in Kafka, given the distributed architecture.

Given these challenges, some possible solutions might include:

1. For **Data Mapping**, businesses should use a metadata management tool, to map the different topics and partitions where a person's data might lie within Kafka.

2. For **Right of Access**, using Kafka Streams API for creating individual state stores per partition or GlobalKTable for maintaining a full replica of the data could simplify providing access.

3. For **Right to be Forgotten**, consider other storage options or using Kafka's log compaction feature. Log compaction ensures that Kafka always retains the last known value for each message key, so if you publish a null value for a key, it effectively deletes all earlier values.

4. For **Data Minimization**, create schemas for the payload and enforce those schemas at the producer level. Schema Registry can help in this process by providing centralized schema management.

5. For **Consent Management**, storing the consent-related decision and processing the data through Kafka Streams based on these decisions could be one solution.

6. For **Data Security**, using SSL for client connection, enabling SASL for client authentication, and using ACL (Access Control Lists) for authorization can ensure security. Kafka also supports data encryption with protocols like SSL/TLS and SASL.

An indirect approach to address these compliance challenges is to have a separate layer in the system architecture that inspects and modifies (if required) the data before it gets into Kafka. Apache

NiFi or StreamSets could be leveraged to build this layer. This layer could also be extended to manage consents from users, by enabling or disabling data processing at an individual level. This layer can ensure that only the necessary and consented data is flowing into Kafka, thereby limiting the scope of GDPR and CCPA.

A final word of caution, this is an emerging and evolving area, and specific solutions could vary based on the organization's infrastructure, architecture and data needs. Consult with legal and data privacy experts while implementing the solution.

6.20   How would you design a Kafka-based system to handle billions of events per second, ensuring both real-time processing and long-term storage?

Designing a Kafka-based system to handle billions of events per second while ensuring both real-time processing and long-term storage entails a variety of considerations including event partitioning, topic replication, producer and consumer group design, stream processing, and integration with a distributed, fault-tolerant storage system like Apache Hadoop HDFS or Amazon S3.

1. Partitioned Topics:

Topics in Kafka are divided into partitions. Each partition can be placed on a separate machine to allow for multiple consumers to read from a topic in parallel. High throughput can thus be achieved by increasing the number of topic partitions and distributing them across multiple brokers.

```
# create a topic with a large number of partitions
kafka-topics.sh --create --zookeeper localhost:2181 --replication-factor 3 --
    partitions 100 --topic my-big-topic
```

2. Topic Replication:

Kafka provides in-built topic replication to achieve fault tolerance and durability. It creates multiple copies of the same partition and stores it in multiple brokers. If a broker goes down, another broker having a copy of the partition takes over processing.

3. Producer Design:

Producers should ensure they evenly distribute traffic across all partitions for load balancing. Kafka's default partitioner can do this.

```
Properties props = new Properties();
// ...
props.put("partitioner.class", "org.apache.kafka.clients.producer.
    RoundRobinPartitioner");
Producer<String, String> producer = new KafkaProducer<>(props);
```

4. Consumer Groups:

Kafka consumers are typically grouped together to consume data in parallel. The number of consumer groups can be increased to accommodate higher throughput.

5. Streaming Data Processing:

Kafka Streams can be used to process the data in real-time as it arrives at the Kafka cluster.

6. Integration with Long-Term Storage:

For long-term data storage, Kafka can be configured to archive data to Hadoop HDFS or Amazon S3. This involves the setup of Apache Kafka Connect, a service provided with Kafka for integrating with other systems.

```
{
  "connector.class": "io.confluent.connect.s3.S3SinkConnector",
  "tasks.max": "10",
  "topics": "my-big-topic",
  // ...
}
```

7. Tweaking Kafka Configuration:

Kafka's settings like segment size, log retention time, and many other broker configurations can be tweaked to optimize for larger amounts of data.

Remember, creating a system to handle billions of events per second is more than just technology; it requires precise capacity planning, thorough testing, and performance tuning. Your Kafka-based system's design, therefore, should be driven by your specific use case requirements.

www.ingramcontent.com/pod-product-compliance
Lightning Source LLC
LaVergne TN
LVHW051337050326
832903LV00031B/3589